THE HOUSE OF CHAN COOKBOOK

THE HOUSE OF CHAN

COOKBOOK

BY SOU CHAN

DRAWINGS BY
SIU LAN LOH

DOUBLEDAY & COMPANY, INC., GARDEN CITY, N.Y., 1953

Library of Congress Catalog Card Number: 52–5543

Copyright, 1952, by Sou Chan
All Rights Reserved
Printed in the United States
At the Country Life Press, Garden City, N.Y.

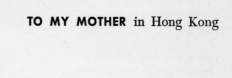

TO MY MOTHER in Hong Kong

Life, like a cookie jar,
would soon be
empty if you continued
to accept the good things
it offers and put in no
good things in return.

WHY I WRITE THIS COOKBOOK

It is rather unexpected for someone like myself to get all these recipes together in a book form which I hope may be use by many of you.

When I landed at Seattle, Washington, in 1928 from China, all my aim was in hoping someday I can run a restaurant of my own somewhere in this country. Today not only my dream came true as a restaurant owner but by completed this cooking directory in Chinese as well.

Cooking and serving food is my most desirable occupation. During my twenty-three years in my adopted country, practically all my time has been with food, either in the kitchen or directly contact with the restaurant goer. Therefore, I have the opportunity to learn to know the desire and otherwise among the American friends, particularly in food. Furthermore, after the fifteen years The House of Chan standing since I start it, now serving average over one thousand friendly customers a day. All these years gave me the additional more close feeling on Chinese cooking. And I dare to say, my restaurant has been introduced more variety of New Chinese dishes to my customers than any other place in this country since the Chinese restaurant been existed. These dishes not newly invented, but has been cooking and serving in the old country for years by the common people daily.

Naturally, I was terrible flatter when I am ask to write a cookbook. Not because for myself, but it is a highly compliment for the food we served. But I wasn't too enthuse about it when I think of writing it because I know there are many Chinese cookbook already been in the public's hand.

Then I gave a second thought about so many friends has came to my restaurant daily from everywhere in this country. I can recall these years there were many friends coming in with their wife and children to enjoy my cooking. During these time, often I received such a remark as "Oh, the Egg Roll and Spareribs are so delicious. I wish we could make them at home so we don't have to come from hundreds of mile for it." I told them sure they could do it and without difficulty at all. Also, I told them—in fact, most Chinese popular dishes are originated from home and large family. But they seems can't be convinced can be done in their own home because they think the ingredients are none obtainable. I tell them in fact most if not all can be found from their corner grocery or vegetable store. May be one or two items can't be bought outside of a

Chinatown, but for these are American type ingredients can be substitute just as well.

Often I try to proof my friends how easy can be cook a Chinese meal at home. So I prepared many recipes to them and also list the substitute items with them. Since then, I had received so many letters telling me how wonderful success they had with my recipes even with substitute ingredients.

Because of this, leads me to change mind and idea of getting this book together in hoping many more friends can be enjoy the same as those has tried. This is why in this book I give separated page of substitution list as a guide to Chinese items as close as possible.

Now, I like to tell you something else is quite important. In Chinese meal is a great difference in compare with American meals in serving. Usually the American meal are consist of one main course and several other side dish such as vegetable, salad and etc. But Chinese meal are consist three or four main course, all equal important. Beside many appetizers serve beforehand, and always serve plain or pan brown rice with other food. So please bear in mind, if you want to serve only one Chinese dish as a main course, you should increase amount ingredients in it more than in recipes. But if you want to serve a more complete Chinese meal, then you will find amounts right for number of people to be served.

You may be kind to think I am an expert in Chinese cooking after you read this, but I am sure you will notice am not an expert in English writing. Therefore, although you are reading this upside down English in this introduction, but you are not going to have same trouble reading recipes, because I was fortunate enough to have a friend of mine, Florence Brobeck, to help me to straighten the writing.

Anyway, please accept my deepest hope you will get a great enjoyment out of this cookbook.

All measurements are level

Most ingredients
are available
in American grocery stores and markets.

CONTENTS

Deep-Fried Chicken Livers
Egg Rolls
Savory Chicken Wings
Etc.

Beef and Watercress Soup
Chicken Soup Yatka Mein
Corn Chowder with Crushed
  Chicken
Soufflé Crab Soup
Etc.

Flounder in Savory Sauce
Friendly Get-Together Supper
Crab Meat with Eggs
Fresh Crabs, Cantonese Style
Barbecued Shrimp
Sweet-and-Sour Shrimp
Etc.

Chicken Roasted in Salt
Chicken with Almonds

誰知盤中餐
粒粒皆辛苦

Rice

FIRST THINGS COME FIRST

> *"Even the humble grain of rice
> would not be, save for the toil of
> man and the bounty of nature."*

Use long-grain rice. Two cups raw rice will make 6 cups cooked rice.

Use a heavy-bottom aluminum pot with tight-fitting lid. It should be tall and deep, not broad and shallow.

Pour cold water over the rice; use your hand to lift and wash the grains. Drain off the starchy water. Pour fresh cold water onto the rice and continue washing and draining as described until the water remains clear. Drain off final washing water, then pour enough cold water into the kettle to cover the rice about 1 inch. Or lay your hand lightly on top of the rice and pour cold water in to barely cover the back of the hand. Or for 2 cups rice use 3 cups water.

Cover the pot tightly. Bring to boiling. As soon as

19

steam escapes, let the rice cook 3 minutes, then turn the heat down halfway. Let cook 2 minutes longer, then turn the heat as low as possible and let the pot stand 15 minutes over this very low heat. The rice is then ready to serve.

Do not be afraid of cooking too much rice. This delicious food is served with every Chinese dish, and leftover rice is used in many dishes.

CHICKEN
FRIED RICE

2 tablespoons oil or bacon fat
1½ cups diced cooked chicken
1 teaspoon salt
½ teaspoon pepper
1 egg
6 cups cooked rice
3 tablespoons soya sauce
1 or 2 scallions, chopped green and white

Heat oil or fat in a frying pan; add chicken; season with salt and pepper. Stir and cook till hot and browning. Add the egg; stir till the cooked egg is in shreds throughout the chicken. Add the rice; stir and cook till browning. Add soya sauce. Mix and cook about 2 minutes. Sprinkle scallions on top, stir, and serve at once. 4 servings.

VARIATIONS

HAM FRIED RICE   In place of chicken in the Chicken Fried Rice recipe use 1½ cups diced boiled or baked ham. Omit salt from recipe.

PORK FRIED RICE   In place of chicken in the above recipe use 1½ cups diced roast pork.

SHRIMP FRIED RICE   In place of chicken in the Chicken Fried Rice recipe use 1½ cups chopped cooked or canned shrimp.

> *Note: Other leftover cooked meats may be used; add ½ cup diced onions or ½ cup canned (or fresh if available) bean sprouts to the mixture.*

SUBGUM FRIED RICE   This means a more elaborate mixture with additions to the Chicken Fried Rice recipe such as ¼ cup diced canned mushrooms, ¼ cup diced green pepper, ½ cup diced onions, ¼ cup diced canned water chestnuts as well as the chicken. Or substitute meat, fish, or shellfish for the chicken.

VEGETABLE SUBGUM FRIED RICE Omit chicken in the Chicken Fried Rice recipe. Add whatever vegetables are available, such as:

> 1 canned pimiento, diced
> 2 green peppers, diced
> 1 cup bean sprouts, canned or fresh
> 1 cup diced celery

The proportion should be 6 cups rice and 3 cups mixed vegetables. Follow the recipe as given.

玉川品茶

Tea~all through the meal

玉
川
品
茶

TO MAKE TEA CHINESE STYLE

Oolong tea from Formosa is the best of the many kinds
of mild, semi-dark tea available. It is naturally sweet
and well flavored and requires no sugar.

To make tea Chinese style, rinse a crockery or china
pot with boiling water. Put 2 tablespoons tea in the
pot for every 4 cups water, or ⅜ teaspoon tea for each
cup. Pour boiling water over it; cover the pot; let stand
3 to 5 minutes. Serve in small cups with meals.

Keep tea in a tightly covered can in a cool, dry place.

閒來獨酌小院

Appetizers

閒
來
獨
酌
小
院

BARBECUED
SPARERIBS

1 clove garlic, mashed
½ cup soya sauce
⅓ cup sugar
1 teaspoon salt
¼ teaspoon pepper
2½ or 3-pound piece young spare-
    ribs (whole piece)
1 tablespoon grated orange peel

Mix garlic, soya sauce, sugar, salt, pepper, and orange peel. Trim fat from spareribs; do not chop or break; use the piece whole. Place meat in a shallow dish or pan, pour the garlic sauce over it and spread over meat. Let stand in the refrigerator about ½ to 1 hour. Turn the meat two or three times in that time, spreading the sauce over it thoroughly each time.

To barbecue in the broiler, place the meat curved side down on a rack in a baking pan. Preheat the broiler 15 minutes; place the rib pan 6 to 8 inches from medium flame for about 20 minutes. When the meat is crusty and done on one side, turn it and continue the cooking till the other side is browned. Total cooking time is 40 to 50 minutes, depending on how hot broiler is. 4 servings.

BUTTERFLY SHRIMP

1½ pounds large fresh shrimp
4 or 5 strips lean bacon cut 1½ inches crosswise
2 egg whites
½ teaspoon salt
4 tablespoons flour
1 or 2 tablespoons cooking oil

Wash and shell shrimp; rinse and drain. With a sharp knife cut a gash down the back of each shrimp, remove dark vein, then make a few gashes crosswise on each shrimp. Mix the egg whites, salt, and flour smoothly. In the long cut of each shrimp apply a thin coat of this mixture. Then lay the bacon strip on top of the mixture and press lightly with your palm. Heat the oil in frying pan. Lay the shrimp bacon side down in the hot pan and sauté on low heat till the bacon is cooked and almost crisp. Turn carefully with a wide spatula; cook other side. When red, serve on toothpicks. 4 or more servings.

TO SERVE AS A MAIN DISH After the shrimp are cooked, add to the hot fat in the frying pan 2 small onions chopped fine; cook till golden, then add ½ cup catchup and 1 cup hot water or chicken stock. Stir and cook till steaming. Thicken, if desired, with 1 tablespoon cornstarch mixed with 3 tablespoons cold water. Pour over the shrimp.

CHINESE
ROAST PORK

> 1 clove garlic
> ½ cup soya sauce
> ¼ cup sugar
> 1 teaspoon salt
> 2 pounds fresh pork butt or
>   shoulder

Mash the garlic with a wooden mallet; mix with soya sauce, sugar, and salt. Cut the meat in 3 lengthwise pieces. Lay the meat in a shallow dish, pour the garlic mixture over it and spread it over the meat. Let stand in the refrigerator about 1 hour. Turn the meat 2 or 3 times in this period. Remove the pork from the dish; lay the pieces on a rack in an uncovered pan. Preheat broiler 15 minutes; place the pan 6 to 8 inches below medium broiler heat. Bake 30 minutes, or till one side is crisp; turn the meat, add a little of the remaining sauce, and continue cooking till the second side is crisp. Total cooking time is 1 to 1½ hours. Too long cooking dries the meat, but it must be thoroughly cooked. Serve hot or cold. It is crusty and delicious. 4 servings.

Note: If oven is used instead of broiler, heat oven, 350° F., and bake 1½ to 2 hours, or till pork is thoroughly cooked.

CHICKEN LIVERS SAUTÉ

1 pound chicken livers
2 or 3 cups boiling water
½ lemon
2 tablespoons soya sauce
¼ cup Oyster Sauce bought, or see recipe
1 cup hot water or chicken stock
½ teaspoon salt
2 teaspoons sugar
2 teaspoons cornstarch
2 tablespoons cold water
1 or 2 scallions, chopped green and white
2 tablespoons minced fine Virginia ham or crushed toasted almonds (optional)

Rinse livers; place in saucepan; add boiling water to

cover. Squeeze half lemon into the water then drop it into the pan. Cover; let heat to boiling point; shut off the heat and let stand 5 minutes. Drain, rinse under running cold water; drain again. Slice the livers lengthwise.

Mix the soya sauce, Oyster Sauce, water or chicken stock, salt, and sugar. Heat to boiling. Add livers and cook 2 or 3 minutes, or till just cooked through. Thicken the sauce in the pan with the cornstarch mixed with 2 tablespoons water; stir and cook 2 or 3 minutes. Add scallions and ham, or almonds, stir, and pour over the livers. 4 or more servings.

DEEP-FRIED CHICKEN LIVERS

> 1 pound chicken livers
> 2 or 3 cups boiling water
> ½ lemon
> 2 cups soya sauce
> ½ teaspoon cinnamon, or small piece cinnamon stick
> 6 tablespoons sugar
> Oil for deep frying
> Minced scallions, green part only, and finely chopped toasted almonds if available

Rinse chicken livers; drain. Squeeze the half lemon into 2 or 3 cups boiling water, then drop it into the

33

water. Add livers. The water should just cover them. Cover and let come to boiling point. Remove from heat, let stand 5 minutes, then drain. Rinse under running cold water. Drain again. In a saucepan mix soya sauce, cinnamon, and sugar. Add chicken livers. Heat slowly, and let simmer 30 minutes. Do not boil. Drain. Heat oil in a deep frying pan. Fry the livers quickly. Serve hot. They should be crusty outside. Serve on a warm dish. Sprinkle with minced scallions and almonds. 4 or more servings.

EGG ROLLS

FILLING

½ cup minced celery
1 cup finely shredded cabbage
2 tablespoons cooking oil
½ cup diced cooked or canned shrimp
½ cup diced roast pork, ham, or beef
½ cup shredded canned bamboo shoots, optional
½ cup shredded canned water chestnuts, optional
2 scallions, minced green and white
1 teaspoon salt
½ teaspoon pepper
3 tablespoons soya sauce

Place celery and cabbage in about ½ cup boiling water; cover and cook till steaming. Drain at once; roll in clean towel; press well to remove as much moisture as possible. Heat oil in a frying pan and cook shrimp and meat 2 or 3 minutes; stir. Add celery, cabbage, bamboo shoots, water chestnuts, scallions, salt, pepper, and soya sauce. Stir till delicately golden all over. Let cool.

PASTRY   The best Egg Roll skins are made with a mixture of Chinese water chestnut flour and wheat flour. If you can shop at a Chinese grocery store, you can buy the skins ready made.

Or use the Western recipe for Puff Paste, roll paper thin, and use as directed below.

OR FOLLOW THIS RECIPE:

> 2 cups sifted flour
> 2 tablespoons cornstarch
> 1 teaspoon salt
> 1 egg, beaten
> 1 teaspoon sugar
> 4 cups water
> Oil for pan or griddle
> 1 tablespoon flour mixed with
> 2 tablespoons water

Sift the flour, cornstarch, and salt together; beat in the egg and sugar; gradually beat in enough water to

35

make a smooth, thin batter. Rub 6-inch pan or small griddle lightly with oil. Set over low heat. Beat batter and pour about 4 tablespoons into the center of the pan. Tilt the pan to spread batter over the entire surface. This makes a very thin pancake. (Pour off excess batter if any.) As soon as the cake shrinks away from the sides of the pan, use fingers, quickly pick it up at one side and carefully turn it over. Let it cook on the other side. Remove from pan; place on plate.

To roll, lay the cooked paste or pancake on the table or a big plate. Place 3 or 4 tablespoons of filling on each. Spread the filling lengthwise, then fold the pastry edge which is along the length of the filling over the filling, then fold one end over this, then the other end, and last, moisten the edge of the remaining side with flour mixed with water. Fold this over the roll and press lightly together.

Both filling and egg roll skin should be completely cold before the roll is made. It would tear easily if still warm.

TO FRY   Heat about 2 inches cooking oil in a 10-inch deep skillet. When hot, place the rolls carefully in the skillet and fry till golden on all sides. Lift out, drain, and serve hot with English mustard, or a mustard sauce and Plum Sauce (also called Duck Sauce). This makes 8 or more rolls. 8 servings.

FRINGE PIKE

> 3 to 4-pound pike, or 1½ pounds pike fillets
> 2 tablespoons Oyster Sauce, bought, or see recipe
> 2 teaspoons soya sauce
> 4 long, thin scallions, white only, cut in 1-inch lengths
> 1 teaspoon sugar
> ⅛ teaspoon pepper
> 1 cup boiling water or fish stock
> ½ cup sliced fresh or canned mushrooms
> 1 teaspoon shredded green ginger root (optional)
> 1 teaspoon cornstarch
> 1 tablespoon cold water

Clean the fish, skin it, and cut fillets off. Cut in 1-inch cubes. Mix all ingredients but cornstarch and water; bring slowly to boiling point, stirring well. Let cook 2 or 3 minutes; add fish; cook 2 or 3 minutes. Mix cornstarch and water together and stir into the fish mixture till slightly thickened. Serve at once. Don't let fish overcook. It continues to cook in its sauce after removing from the range. As a small side "on the fringe" appetizer at a banquet, this makes 8 to 10 servings.

FAN-TAIL
SHRIMP

1 pound large fresh shrimp
  (15 to 18 per pound)
1 teaspoon sugar
¼ cup flour
½ teaspoon salt
¼ teaspoon pepper
1 egg
Oil for deep frying
Plum Sauce. See recipe

Wash shrimp, shell them, leave tail on. Clean out vein, wash, and drain. Cut a slit through the middle of each shrimp; turn the tail up and pull through the slit.

Sift the sugar, flour, salt, and pepper together; beat the egg slightly; mix all together. Dip shrimp in this; place in frying basket, lower into hot oil, and fry till golden. Serve hot with Plum Sauce (also called Duck Sauce). 4 or more servings.

STUFFED
FROGS' LEGS

1 pound large frogs' legs,
  cleaned and chilled
¼ pound Virginia ham
1 or 2 egg whites
2 or 3 tablespoons flour

½ teaspoon salt
¼ teaspoon pepper
Oil for deep frying

Break and remove bone of each frog leg. Cut ham in
very slender sticks and insert in each leg in the bone
cavity. Beat egg whites slightly, mix with flour and
seasonings. Dip frogs' legs in this, then fry in deep hot
oil till light golden and crusty. Serve hot with soya
sauce or Plum Sauce (see recipe). 4 or more servings.

SAVORY
CHICKEN WINGS

8 chicken wings
2 or 3 cups boiling water
½ lemon
2 tablespoons soya sauce
¼ cup Oyster Sauce, bought, or
see recipe
1 cup hot water or chicken stock
4½ teaspoons salt
2 teaspoons sugar
1 tablespoon powdered
cinnamon
½ tablespoon powdered ginger
¼ teaspoon pepper

Rinse wings; cut off tips and discard. Place wings in
a saucepan, just barely cover with boiling water.

Squeeze the half lemon into the pan, then drop it in. Cover and bring to boiling point. Lower heat; simmer 5 minutes; drain. Cover with the mixed soya sauce, Oyster Sauce, hot water or stock, ½ teaspoon salt, and sugar; bring to boiling, lower the heat, and cook 20 minutes, or till done. Drain; let cool. Mix the remaining 4 teaspoons salt, the cinnamon, ginger, and pepper in a small frying pan or chafing dish. Stir or shake till hot; dip the wings in till coated; serve. 4 or 8 servings.

作羹調味

Soups

作羹調味

BEEF AND
WATERCRESS
SOUP

2 cups fresh watercress
Salt
½ pound finely ground or diced
lean beef
1 tablespoon soya sauce
1 teaspoon chicken fat or
cooking oil
3 cups boiling water
3 cups chicken stock
1 drop sesame seed oil

Wash cress, cut off heavy stems; drain. Fill a pan with cold water; add 2 tablespoons salt; stir it, then add the watercress. Let stand half an hour. Drain; rinse thoroughly under running cold water.

Place meat in a bowl with soya sauce, fat or oil, and about 1 teaspoon salt. Mix well and let stand 20 minutes. Bring stock and water to boiling point; add the watercress, stir, and when boiling begins again, add the sesame seed oil, then the meat. Stir and serve at once. 4 servings.

Note: Chinese taste prefers all foods cooked as little as possible; in the recipe above the hot soup continues to cook the meat even after the heat is turned off.

BEEF VEGETABLE SOUP

½ pound (2 cups) lean beef, diced
1 teaspoon salt
2 tablespoons soya sauce
1 tablespoon cooking oil or chicken fat
6 cups boiling water or chicken stock
2 cups mixed raw vegetables which include diced cabbage, chopped celery, and either raw spinach leaves cut in halves or chopped chard
1 drop sesame seed oil

Combine beef, salt, soya sauce, and oil or chicken fat.

Mix well. Let stand 20 or 30 minutes. Heat water or stock. When boiling add the mixed vegetables, stir, and when boiling add the drop of sesame oil, then the meat; stir and bring to boiling point again. Serve at once. 4 servings.

CELERY CABBAGE SOUP

2 tablespoons cooking oil
1 tablespoon soya sauce
1 teaspoon salt
½ teaspoon pepper
½ pound beef, chopped or cut in
  very small, very thin slices
6 cups water or chicken stock
½ pound celery cabbage,
  chopped fine
1 drop sesame seed oil
1 or 2 young scallions, chopped
  green and white

Mix oil, soya sauce, salt, and pepper, and spread over the meat; let stand in the refrigerator 1 hour or longer. Heat water or stock. When boiling add celery cabbage. Stir, and when boiling again add the sesame seed oil and meat. Stir and let come to boiling point. Add scallions, stir, and serve at once. 4 servings.

45

CHICKEN
STOCK

Bones of 1 chicken
7 cups water
Salt

Cover bones with cold water. Cover the kettle and cook slowly, over low heat, 1 to 1½ hours. Let it cool; skim fat from top. Reheat stock and use with rice or noodles, or in other recipes. Makes 4 to 6 cups.

Note: Leftover turkey bones may be used in place of chicken.

CHICKEN
BROTH
AND
NOODLES

6 cups chicken stock
1 cup thin, fine dry noodles, broken
1 teaspoon salt
2 quarts boiling water
2 teaspoons soya sauce
1 scallion, minced green and white
½ cup shredded cooked chicken, optional

Heat stock slowly. Drop noodles into salted boiling

46

water. Boil rapidly 10 minutes; drain in colander; rinse under cold-water faucet; drain again. Add noodles to boiling stock. Stir, bring to boiling point again; add soya sauce, scallion, and chicken. Stir to mix. Serve at once. 4 to 6 servings.

CHICKEN BROTH WITH EGG CUBES AND RICE

6 cups chicken stock
2 eggs
½ teaspoon sugar
1 teaspoon salt
¼ teaspoon pepper
1 or 2 scallions, chopped green and white
1 tablespoon cooking oil
1 cup cooked rice

Heat stock slowly. Beat eggs, sugar, salt, pepper, and scallions together. Heat oil in very small frying pan; turn egg mixture into pan; cook as for omelet. When bottom is cooked, turn the omelet and cook the other side. Let cool; cut in small squares. Add rice to boiling stock; stir, pour into cups. Garnish with diced omelet. 4 to 6 servings.

47

CHICKEN
EGG DROP
SOUP

6 cups chicken stock
3 tablespoons cornstarch
3 tablespoons cold water
½ teaspoon sugar
1 teaspoon salt
¼ teaspoon pepper
2 eggs, beaten
2 or 3 scallions, chopped green
and white

Heat stock to boiling point; mix cornstarch smoothly with water; add sugar, salt, and pepper; stir slowly into the stock till smoothly blended and boiling. Reduce heat; add beaten eggs; stir slowly about 1 or 2 minutes till the eggs separate in shreds. Turn off heat. Add scallions, stir, and serve at once. 4 servings.

TOMATO
EGG DROP
SOUP

6 cups chicken stock
2 cups canned or 1 cup chopped
fresh tomatoes
2 tablespoons cornstarch
¼ cup cold water

48

1 teaspoon sugar
1 teaspoon salt
¼ teaspoon pepper
2 eggs, beaten

Heat stock to boiling point; stir in tomatoes; bring to
boiling point; cover; let simmer 2 or 3 minutes. Mix
cornstarch smoothly with water, sugar, salt, and pepper. Stir slowly into the hot tomato soup. When
smooth and boiling reduce the heat; add the beaten
eggs. Stir about 1 or 2 minutes till the eggs separate in
shreds. Turn off heat. Serve at once. 4 servings.

CHICKEN
SOUP
YATKA MEIN
BOWL OF NOODLES

6 cups chicken stock
1 pound very thin, dry noodles
(do not break)
Boiling water
1 cup shredded cooked chicken
1 drop sesame seed oil in each
bowl
2 hard-cooked eggs, cut in
halves
6 tablespoons minced scallions,
green and white

49

Heat stock slowly. Drop noodles into salted boiling water. Boil rapidly 10 minutes, or till tender. Drain in colander; rinse under cold-water faucet; drain. Add to hot stock; bring to boiling point. Pour the shredded chicken in on top of the noodles. Serve at once in bowls containing 1 drop sesame seed oil. To each serving add ½ hard-cooked egg and 1 tablespoon minced scallions. 4 servings.

> *Note: This dish is a one-dish meal for a light lunch or midnight snack.*

ROAST PORK SOUP YATKA MEIN Use shredded roast pork in place of the chicken in the preceding recipe. Add 1 tablespoon soya sauce to boiling stock.

LETTUCE EGG DROP SOUP Omit scallions from Egg Drop Soup. Add 1½ cups washed lettuce leaves chopped fine to the hot egg soup. Stir lettuce in and serve at once. Do not let boil after lettuce is added. 4 servings.

CORN CHOWDER WITH CRUSHED CHICKEN Make Crushed Corn Soup (see following recipe) but omit the 1 egg called for in that recipe.

> 1 cup crushed raw white chicken meat
> 2 egg whites

Grind the chicken meat as fine as possible, putting it through the grinder 2 or 3 times. Then pound or mash to smoothness with mallet or wooden potato masher. Beat the egg whites slightly; mix with crushed chicken. Stir into the boiling corn soup. Bring to boiling point again, then reduce heat and cook slowly 10 minutes. Scatter Virginia ham or almonds over it and serve at once. 4 servings.

CRUSHED CORN SOUP

> 1 can kernel corn or 2 cups
>   cooked sweet corn
> 1 egg, beaten
> 1 teaspoon cornstarch
> 2 tablespoons cold water
> 1 tablespoon salt
> ½ teaspoon pepper
> 6 cups boiling chicken stock
> 1 or 2 tablespoons crushed
>   Virginia ham or crushed
>   toasted almonds

Put corn through fine grinder; stir egg into corn. Mix cornstarch smoothly with the water; add to corn; add seasonings. Mix well, then stir slowly into the boiling stock. Cover pot and bring soup to boiling point. Turn heat low and let simmer 2 or 3 minutes. Remove cover;

scatter Virginia ham or almonds over all. Serve at once. 4 servings.

EGG CUBE SOUP

6 cups chicken stock
1 teaspoon sugar
2 teaspoons soya sauce
3 eggs
½ teaspoon salt
¼ teaspoon pepper
1 scallion, chopped green and white
1 tablespoon cooking oil

Heat stock slowly. Beat the eggs slightly; season with salt and pepper; add chopped scallion. Pour into a small hot frying pan containing the tablespoon of oil. When the omelet is cooked on the underside, turn, and cook the other side; let cool. Cut in small cubes. Stir sugar and soya sauce into the boiling stock. Stir, add egg cubes, and serve at once. 4 to 6 servings.

PIKE SOUP

FISH STOCK

Bones, head, and tail of 1 large pike
1 teaspoon salt
¼ teaspoon pepper

5 cups cold water

½ cup thinly sliced canned or fresh mushrooms or 1 or 2 tablespoons minced celery leaves

3 teaspoons cornstarch, optional

Place the pike head, tail, and bones with a little meat left on them in a kettle with salt, pepper, and water. Cover the pot; bring slowly to boiling point; reduce the heat and let simmer. Do not let the steam escape; the flavor is in the steam. Cook slowly ½ hour after it comes to boiling. Add mushrooms or celery leaves. Cook 1 or 2 minutes longer. If clear soup is preferred, ladle off and serve at once. If thickened soup is preferred, strain the soup before adding mushrooms or celery leaves. Stir the cornstarch into 2 tablespoons cold water, add to the soup. Stir while it boils 2 or 3 minutes, then serve at once. 4 servings.

SOUFFLÉ
CRAB SOUP

6 cups chicken stock
½ teaspoon salt
¼ teaspoon pepper
1 cup cooked or canned crab
  meat
2 eggs, beaten
1 tablespoon cornstarch
¼ cup cold water
½ head tender green lettuce,
  chopped fine

Heat stock; add seasoning if necessary. Look over crab meat and remove any cartilage. Beat eggs lightly, stir quickly into the boiling stock; add cornstarch mixed with the water; stir; boil 1 or 2 minutes; add crab meat and lettuce. Stir. Serve at once. 4 servings.

SHRIMP
SOUP

½ pound fresh shrimp
2 egg whites
1 or 2 thin slices ground or
  mashed young ginger root
1 cup chopped raw cabbage
½ cup chopped celery
1 teaspoon salt

6 cups boiling water
2 tablespoons cornstarch
3 tablespoons cold water
1 or 2 scallions, chopped green
and white
½ cup chopped raw spinach

Shell and clean shrimp; remove vein, rinse, and drain; grind shrimp very fine and smooth. Beat egg whites lightly; mix with shrimp and ginger. Cook cabbage and celery in salted boiling water 10 minutes. Mix cornstarch smoothly with the cold water; stir into the cooked vegetables. Bring to boiling point. Stir 1 or 2 minutes. Add the shrimp, stir, bring to boiling point again, and cook 5 minutes. Add the scallions and spinach, stir, and serve at once. 4 servings.

WON TON SOUP   This soup requires time in preparation, because the Won Tons, or small filled dumpling-like additions to the soup, must be prepared carefully. First the

WON TON SKIN

2 cups flour
1 teaspoon salt
1 large egg
⅛ cup water

Sift flour and salt into a mixing bowl. Beat egg slightly;

stir into flour; add water a few drops at a time, mixing just until dough is right for rolling. Turn dough out on lightly floured board; kneed until smooth, turning it and folding over several times. Cover lightly with clean towel; let stand on the board about 20 minutes. Roll out as thin as possible (paper-thin); cut in 2-inch squares.

In center of each square place a small amount of filling (see below). Fold each square in triangle shape; press edges together but leave point of triangle open a little.

WON TON
FILLING

> 1 pound finely ground pork
> 1 egg, beaten
> 1 tablespoon soya sauce
> ½ teaspoon salt
> ¼ teaspoon pepper

Mix pork and remaining ingredients smoothly together. Use as filling as described above.

> *Note: For a "Friday filling" omit pork; use chopped shrimp or fish.*

WON TON SOUP

Boiling salted water
20 raw Won Tons
6 cups chicken stock
Seasoning, if needed
2 tablespoons chopped scallions,
   optional
2 tablespoons soya sauce

Place Won Tons in boiling water and cook till they float to the surface; remove with slotted spoon; drain.

Heat stock; add seasoning if needed. If vegetables are used in stock, a small amount of celery cabbage, bok choy, spinach, or similar tender leafy vegetables are fine. Be sure that these are not overcooked. Place Won Tons in 4 or 5 bowls; sprinkle with scallions, add a little soya sauce; pour hot stock over Won Tons. Serve at once. 4 or 5 servings.

Fish & Shellfish

山珍海味

FILLET
OF PIKE

2½-pound pike or 2 pounds pike
  fillets
3 tablespoons cooking oil
1 teaspoon salt
½ teaspoon pepper
1 thin slice green ginger root or
  ½ teaspoon powdered ginger,
  optional
1 can (2 cups) bean sprouts or
  1 pound fresh sprouts
2 tablespoons soya sauce
1 cup scallions, cut in 1-inch
  pieces
2 tablespoons cornstarch
¼ cup cold water

If you buy whole pike, cut off head and tail and skin
it. (Use these and the bones for fish stock, if desired.)

Cut fillets off the bones and cut them crosswise in ⅛ inch thick pieces. Heat oil, salt, pepper, and ginger and add fish. Sauté a few minutes; remove to a hot plate. Add the bean sprouts to the liquid; cook 2 minutes after boiling. Add fish to the sprouts, soya sauce, and scallions. Stir; bring to boiling point; cook 1 or 2 minutes. Mix cornstarch and cold water; stir into the fish mixture; cook till the sauce is thickened. Serve at once. 4 servings.

FISHERMAN'S SEA BASS

2-pound very fresh sea bass
1½ teaspoons salt
4 tablespoons soya sauce
¼ lemon peel, shredded thin as hair or grated
1 or 2 very thin slices green ginger root or 1 teaspoon powdered ginger
¼ teaspoon powdered cinnamon
3 or 4 slender scallions, cut in long pieces and split
½ cup cooking oil

Scale, clean, and wash fish, but leave it whole. Leave head on and make sure the eyes of the fish are round and full. Preheat an oval pan about the same size as the fish. Pour boiling water into it, then lower the fish into the water. Be sure there is enough water to amply cover the fish. Let it stand covered 20 to 25 minutes. When the fish eyes pop up, half out, the fish is almost cooked. Remove the fish gently from the water onto a warm oval platter. Sprinkle salt over the fish, then sprinkle the other ingredients over it. Heat the oil and pour over the fish evenly; the hot oil forces the seasoning into the fish and completes the cooking. 4 servings.

> *Note: Only a very fresh fish can be used in this recipe.*

BLOWFISH TAILS

12 fresh blowfish tails
  (or "sea squab")
6 tablespoons cooking oil
1½ teaspoons salt
½ garlic clove, mashed
3 tablespoons soya sauce
1 tablespoon sherry
2 tablespoons hot water
1 teaspoon sugar
1 or 2 young scallions or onions, minced

Heat oil, garlic, and salt; add tails and brown on one

63

side. Turn the tails to brown. Mix soya sauce, sherry, hot water, and sugar. Pour over the tails; cover the pan and let come to boiling. Add scallions or onions and serve. 4 servings.

Note: These tails are not available in all fish markets, but once tried will be much appreciated for their low cost and good flavor.

FLOUNDER
IN
SAVORY SAUCE

2 ½-pound flounders
2 tablespoons cooking oil
½ teaspoon salt
¼ teaspoon pepper
4 tablespoons soya sauce
2 tablespoons minced green
    scallions
2 tablespoons water

Clean flounders; cut off head and tail. (Use for fish stock, if desired.)

Heat oil, salt, and pepper. Add flounders and sauté 2 or 3 minutes. Pour soya sauce over, sprinkle with the scallions and water. Cover the pan; cook 2 or 3 minutes over low heat. Serve. 4 servings.

PORGIES
IN
SAVORY SAUCE

2 ½ to ¾-pound porgies
4 tablespoons cooking oil
1 teaspoon salt
¼ teaspoon pepper
1 small piece green ginger root,
   mashed, or ½ teaspoon
   powdered ginger, optional
4 tablespoons soya sauce
4 tablespoons water
2 tablespoons minced green
   scallions

Select porgies at the fish market. (They usually are sold ready to cook.) Rinse; drain. Heat oil, salt, pepper, and ginger (if used). Sauté the fish till delicately golden on both sides; pour the soya sauce over them; add water; cover; let simmer 3 to 5 minutes after the boiling point is reached. Add scallions. Serve at once. 2 to 4 servings.

FRIENDLY GET-TOGETHER SUPPER (In Chinese called "DAR BEN LO") This is ideal for a large chafing dish or a casserole placed over canned heat or a small electric plate in the center of a table. Guests and family sit around the table, cooking their own selected food and talking while their food cooks.

65

Around the chafing dish, in decorative Chinese
dishes, place the various foods; in small dishes, such as
butter dishes, pour the flavorful sauces, such as Plum
Sauce (Duck Sauce), Mustard Sauce, and Soya Sauce.
The ingredients for the supper are:

> 8 cups chicken broth
> 12 or more very thin strips raw
>   sturgeon, pike, or red snapper
>   cut 2 inches long, ½ inch thick,
>   and 1 inch wide
> 12 or more very thin strips raw
>   white meat of chicken
> 12 or more very thin strips raw
>   beef
> 4 chicken livers sliced thin or 4
>   small thin slices raw beef liver
> 1 or 2 chicken hearts, split open
> 1 head tender green lettuce,
>   washed and the leaves pulled
>   off
> 3 or 4 young scallions, cut in 1-
>   inch pieces
> 1 cup Chinese celery cabbage,
>   chopped fine
> 1½ tablespoons soya sauce
> 1 drop sesame seed oil

Have the stock boiling in the dish. Guests use their
chopsticks and pick up whatever they want to cook,
then place it in the boiling broth. Each guest watches

his own food cooking and removes it with his chop-sticks to his plate when it is cooked. To eat it he wraps it in a lettuce leaf, adding sauce and scallions if de-sired. When everybody has eaten all he wants, the re-maining stock, which has been deliciously flavored with the fish, chicken, and other foods, is stirred, the cabbage added, and the mixture stirred again and cooked 2 or 3 minutes. Then soya sauce is added, the drop of sesame oil, and the soup is quickly served in small bowls. 6 servings.

> *Note: Any other quick-cooking vegetables, such as spinach, may be used in place of the celery cabbage; fresh crab meat or shrimp may be added to the foods to be cooked. In place of the lettuce leaves, some Chinese guests prefer a thin slice of bread to wrap around the cooked food.*

SMELTS IN SAVORY SAUCE

12 smelts
3 tablespoons cooking oil
½ teaspoon salt
¼ teaspoon pepper
4 tablespoons soya sauce
2 tablespoons minced green
scallions
2 tablespoons water

Clean smelts. Sauté in the hot oil 7 minutes, or till done. Add seasoning; pour soya sauce over them; sprinkle with the scallions and water. Cover the pan; cook 1 or 2 minutes. Serve. 3 or 4 servings.

SAVORY STEAMED WHITEFISH

1½ to 2-pound piece of a large
whitefish
1 teaspoon salt
2 tablespoons soya sauce
1 tablespoon shredded green
ginger root or ½ teaspoon
powdered ginger
2 tablespoons shredded lemon
peel

½ cup sliced canned or fresh
    mushrooms
½ cup shredded ham
2 tablespoons cooking oil or
    chicken fat

With a thin, sharp knife make a cut crosswise in the
skin of the fish in several places, about 1 inch apart.
Lay the fish in a shallow baking dish. Mix the remaining ingredients and spread over the fish. Let marinate,
covered, in the refrigerator 10 to 15 minutes, then set
the dish on a rack in a large kettle. Pour boiling water
in the kettle to within 1 inch of the rack. Cover the
kettle tightly, cook over moderate heat till the water
is boiling, then let steam 30 minutes, or till done. Serve
at once. 4 servings.

RED SNAPPER JAWS

1½ pounds fresh red snapper
    jaws or cheeks
1½ teaspoons salt
½ teaspoon pepper
1 teaspoon powdered ginger,
    optional
4 tablespoons cooking oil
1 cup fish stock or hot water
2 tablespoons soya sauce
4 young scallions, chopped fine

69

Rinse jaws or cheeks; drain; sprinkle with salt, pepper, and ginger, if used. Heat the oil very hot in a frying pan; sauté the fish; cook till golden.

Add the stock or hot water. Cover the pan and let simmer 5 minutes. Stir soya sauce and scallions into the pan. Serve at once. 4 servings.

> *Variation: After sautéing the fish as described, add ½ cup diced mushrooms (previously washed and soaked), ¼ pound pork shoulder shredded, and 2 cups water. Cover; simmer 15 minutes after boiling point is reached. Add peel of 1 orange cut in fine shreds and 1 scallion chopped fine. Stir. Serve. Add, if desired, 1 tablespoon cornstarch mixed with 2 tablespoons water as thickening.*

STURGEON SAUTÉED WITH VEGETABLES

1½ pounds fresh sturgeon fillets
3 tablespoons cooking oil
1 teaspoon salt
½ teaspoon pepper
½ cup sliced fresh or canned
    button mushrooms

> 1 cup bamboo shoots, optional
> 1 cup chopped celery cabbage
> 1 cup bean sprouts, optional
> 1 cup hot water or stock
> 3 tablespoons soya sauce
> 1 tablespoon cornstarch
> ¼ cup cold water

Cut fillets crosswise in ¼-inch strips.

Heat oil, salt, and pepper; sauté the fish 1 or 2 minutes only. Remove to a hot dish. Add the vegetables and water or stock to the pan. Cover; cook 3 to 5 minutes after boiling point is reached. Add fish, and soya sauce mixed with cornstarch and cold water. Stir till thickened. Serve at once. 4 servings.

SHELLFISH

STEAMED LOBSTERS

> 6 live baby lobsters
> Boiling water

Place the lobsters on a rack in a large wide kettle containing 1½ cups boiling water, 4 lobsters on the rack, 2 on top of them. Cover and let cook, low heat, till lobsters are red—about 30 minutes. Remove lobsters; crack claws; split lobster down the underside; remove lung and intestine and discard them.

Add 4 or more tablespoons of butter to the water in the kettle. Stir till butter is melted then pour liquid into 6 small bowls. Each person picks the lobster meat from the shells and dips it into the hot sauce. This method saves all the essence of the lobster. 6 servings.

LOBSTER CANTONESE STYLE

> 2 1-pound live lobsters
> 4 tablespoons oil
> 1 small sliver garlic
> ½ pound ground fresh pork
> 3 tablespoons soya sauce
> 1 teaspoon sugar
> 1 teaspoon salt
> ½ teaspoon pepper
> 1½ cups boiling water
> 1 teaspoon cornstarch
> ¼ cup cold water
> 1 egg
> 4 young scallions, chopped green and white

Wash lobsters, chop off head, remove claws and crack each; clean out lung and intestinal tract and discard them. Cut lobster through shell into halves, then crosswise in 1-inch pieces.

Heat oil and mash garlic into it; add the pork and cook till browned. Pour soya sauce over it; stir. Add sugar, salt, pepper, and boiling water, and mix. Add the lobster and claws. Cover; cook 10 minutes. Mix cornstarch and cold water. Stir into the pan till the sauce is thickened and smooth. Turn off heat. Beat egg slightly, pour over the lobster; stir. Add scallions; stir well. Serve. 4 servings.

SAVORY STEAMED LOBSTERS

> 4 live baby lobsters
> 3 eggs
> 1 teaspoon salt
> ½ teaspoon pepper
> ¼ pound ground pork shoulder
> ¼ cup diced scallions
> 2 tablespoons cooking oil
> 1 teaspoon sugar
> 2 tablespoons soya sauce
> 1 tablespoon sherry

Clean and cut the lobsters as described in Lobster Cantonese Style. Arrange the pieces in a shallow baking dish or platter. Beat eggs slightly; add seasonings and other ingredients; mix thoroughly. Spread this over the lobster. Set the platter on a rack in a large

kettle containing hot water to within 1 inch of the rack.
Cover the kettle. Bring the water to boiling point, then
let boil gently over low heat 35 minutes. Serve hot. 4
servings.

FRESH CRABS, CANTONESE STYLE

2 or 4 large live soft-shell crabs
   or canned crab meat
4 tablespoons cooking oil
1 small sliver garlic
1 teaspoon salt
¼ or ½ pound ground fresh pork
2 tablespoons soya sauce
1 teaspoon sugar
½ teaspoon pepper
1 cup boiling water or stock
1 teaspoon cornstarch
¼ cup cold water
1 egg
2 young scallions, chopped
   green and white

Clean and wash crabs. Cut in 6 or 8 pieces. Heat oil,
mash garlic in a large, heavy frying pan; add the salt
and pork and cook till lightly browned. Pour soya
sauce over it; stir; add sugar, pepper, and boiling

water or stock. Add the crab pieces; stir to mix well; cover; cook over moderate heat 10 minutes.

Mix cornstarch and cold water; stir into the pan till the sauce is thickened and smooth. Turn heat off. Beat the egg slightly; stir into the crab mixture; add scallions. Stir well. Serve at once. 4 servings.

CRAB MEAT WITH EGGS

> 1 pound fresh or quick-frozen crab meat
> 1 small onion, cut in long, thin shreds, or 2 cups drained canned or fresh bean sprouts
> 2 tablespoons cooking oil
> 1 teaspoon salt
> ½ teaspoon pepper
> 6 eggs
> 1 young scallion, cut in 1-inch lengths

Look over crab meat and discard all cartilage. Cook the onion or bean sprouts in the oil till tender; add salt and pepper. Sauté crab meat 3 or 4 minutes, turning with a spatula. Beat eggs, add to pan, and reduce heat; stir and cook till mixture is like light scrambled eggs. Sprinkle with scallion. Serve. 4 servings.

75

BARBECUED
SHRIMP

1 cup soya sauce
½ teaspoon pepper
2 teaspoons salt
¼ cup sugar
1 thin piece green ginger root, mashed, or ½ teaspoon powdered ginger
1 sliver garlic, mashed
2 pounds fresh shrimp
10 strips lean bacon, cut in 4 pieces
1 pound beef liver, sliced thin, same size as bacon pieces
1 loaf fresh French bread, sliced thin, crusts cut off

Shell and clean shrimp. Mix soya sauce, pepper, salt, sugar, ginger, and garlic. Cut a deep gash down the back of the shrimp and spread open wide. Lay a piece of bacon on each shrimp, liver on top. Arrange on a platter. Pour the sauce over. Let marinate 10 to 20 minutes. Drain off sauce. Use long, thin skewers. On each place a shrimp, piece of liver, piece of bacon; repeat till skewers are full. Barbecue over low coals. Turn skewers as often as necessary to cook the food. Push cooked shrimp, liver, and bacon off skewers onto plates. To eat fold a slice of bread around a cooked shrimp, liver, and bacon. 8 to 10 servings.

SHRIMP
WITH TOMATOES
AND
GREEN PEPPER

1 pound fresh shrimp
2 large green peppers
½ garlic clove, mashed
4 tablespoons cooking oil
1 teaspoon salt
¼ teaspoon pepper
1 or 2 thin slices green ginger
  root, mashed, or 1 teaspoon
  powdered ginger, optional
1½ cups hot water or stock
2 tomatoes, cut in quarters or
  sixths
2 tablespoons soya sauce
2 tablespoons cornstarch
¼ cup cold water
3 or 4 slender scallions, chopped
  green and white

Shell and clean shrimp. Rinse and drain; split each shrimp down the back, but not all the way through. Wash peppers; drain; cut in 6 or 8 pieces; discard seeds and fibers.

Heat garlic, oil, salt, pepper, and ginger in a large, heavy frying pan or pot. Add shrimp; cook 2 or 3 minutes, stirring and mixing; add green peppers; stir. Then add water or stock; mix; cover the pan. Bring to boiling point and let cook on moderate heat 3 to 5 minutes. Stir once or twice. Add the tomatoes; mix well; cook 2 or 3 minutes. Mix the soya sauce, cornstarch, and cold water and stir into the shrimp mixture. Cook and stir 1 to 2 minutes till thickened; add the scallions; mix. Serve at once. 4 servings.

SHRIMP
AND
TOMATO SAUCE

> 2 tablespoons cooking oil
> 1 teaspoon salt
> ¼ teaspoon pepper
> 1 pound fresh shrimp
> 1 teaspoon sugar
> 2 or 3 tomatoes, chopped, or
>   2 cups canned tomatoes
> ½ cup hot water or stock
> 1 tablespoon cornstarch
> 2 teaspoons soya sauce
> ¼ cup cold water

Shell and clean shrimp. Heat the oil, salt, and pepper; stir the shrimp in the pan and cook 3 or 4 minutes, or till lightly cooked. Mix sugar and tomatoes and pour over the shrimp. Stir; cook 2 or 3 minutes. Add the hot water or stock slowly, stir, and mix well. Cover the pan, bring to boiling point, then simmer over low heat

3 minutes. Mix cornstarch, soya sauce, and cold water. Stir into the shrimp mixture and cook till the sauce thickens. Serve at once over hot rice. 4 servings.

SWEET-AND-SOUR SHRIMP

	1 pound fresh large shrimp
	Oil for deep frying
BATTER	1 egg
FOR SHRIMP	½ cup sifted flour
	½ teaspoon salt
	2 tablespoons water
SAUCE	1 cup vinegar
	1 cup brown sugar
	1 cup water
	3 tablespoons catchup
	½ teaspoon salt
	¼ teaspoon pepper
	2 cups shredded canned pineapple
	2 large green peppers, each cut diagonally in 8 pieces
	2 large tomatoes, each cut in 6 wedges
	1 tablespoon cornstarch

Wash the shrimp, shell, clean, and drain them. Split

them along the back but do not cut all the way through. Beat the egg; add flour, salt, and water, and beat until smooth. Dip shrimp in the batter; fry in hot oil till golden. Drain.

In a large enamel saucepan put the vinegar, sugar, 1 cup water, catchup, salt, pepper, pineapple, green peppers, and tomatoes. Bring to boiling point. Mix cornstarch and 2 tablespoons water; stir into the sauce; cook till thickened. Add shrimp; heat; stir; mix thoroughly. Cook 1 minute after boiling point is reached. 4 servings.

SHRIMP PATTIES

> ½ pound fresh shrimp, shelled and cleaned
> ½ pound fresh pork shoulder
> 1 teaspoon grated lemon peel
> ½ cup chopped scallions, white and a very little green
> 1 teaspoon salt
> ½ teaspoon pepper
> 2 tablespoons cooking oil
> Soya sauce

Cut the shrimp in pieces, then put through a meat grinder three times with the pork, lemon peel, and scallions. Season with salt and pepper. Beat and pound the mixture till smooth and pasty. Shape in round cakes ½ inch thick. Pan-brown in a little hot oil; press cakes down with spatula; use low heat so that pork in the cakes cooks thoroughly. Turn and brown other side. Serve hot with a dash of soya sauce. 4 to 6 servings.

> *Note: The cooked patties may be cut up and used in place of chicken or beef in vegetable recipes calling for the addition of meat.*

SHRIMP WITH CURRY SAUCE

1 pound fresh jumbo shrimp
4 tablespoons curry powder
1 teaspoon salt
5 tablespoons cooking oil
2 cups boiling water or stock
3 or 4 young scallions, chopped green and white

Rinse shrimp; cut off heads but do not shell them. Heat the curry powder in a hot pan; stir; add salt; gradually add the oil, stirring until smooth. Add shrimp and sauté till shells are golden. Add water or stock gradually, stirring and mixing. Cover, bring to boiling point, and let cook 5 minutes; add scallions; mix; stir till well heated. Serve hot. Eat with fingers. 4 servings.

81

Poultry

CHICKEN
ROASTED IN SALT

4-pound roasting chicken
2 to 4 pounds salt

Draw and wash chicken. Dry thoroughly inside and out by hanging in a cold room, or use soft absorbent paper tissues to wipe it. Pour the salt in a deep, heavy iron pot. Heat and stir till very hot—about 30 minutes. Make a deep impression in the center; set the chicken in the salt. Scoop salt up around the chicken to entirely cover it. Cover the pot tightly. Cook over low heat 30 minutes, then turn heat off and let stand 30 minutes. The chicken will be done. Remove chicken from the salt and let it cool a little—about 20 minutes—before serving. 4 to 6 servings. This is juicy and tender, not salty—a favorite Chinese dish.

Note: The salt can be reused as usual in cookery.

85

CHICKEN
WITH
CURRY SAUCE

3 to 4-pound young hen
1½ teaspoons salt
5 tablespoons cooking oil
6 tablespoons curry powder
2 cups boiling water or stock
3 or 4 young scallions, chopped
green and white

Draw and wash chicken; cut into serving pieces; wipe dry; rub with salt. Heat 3 tablespoons oil in a large, heavy frying pan and cook the chicken till golden. In a smaller pan heat the curry powder; when very hot, add about 2 tablespoons oil, a little at a time, stirring continually until smooth. Gradually add the boiling water or stock, stirring steadily. Let cook till smooth and bubbling. Pour over the chicken; cover the pot; cook over very low heat till the chicken is done—about 1 hour. If sauce is not thick, add about 1 tablespoon cornstarch mixed with ¼ cup cold water. Stir into the sauce till thickened and smooth. Serve sprinkled with scallions and garnished with mounds of hot rice. 4 servings.

Note: In China, curried dishes are eaten only in winter; we heat the curry powder in the hot pan to kill the green flavor. Buy yellow curry powder of even color; poor curry is darker and uneven in color.

CHICKEN
WITH PINEAPPLE

3 tablespoons flour
½ teaspoon salt
¼ teaspoon pepper
3 tablespoons water
2 cups large cubes raw chicken
Oil for deep-fat cooking
3 teaspoons soya sauce
2 rings canned pineapple, cut in
    quarters
8 pieces green pepper, same size
    as pineapple
2 carrots, sliced slantwise as thin
    as possible
1½ cups water
½ cup vinegar
3 tablespoons brown sugar
1 tablespoon molasses
2 tablespoons cornstarch
¼ cup canned pineapple juice

Mix flour, salt, pepper, and water to a smooth batter.
Pour over the chicken. Mix till the chicken is coated,
then place the chicken, a piece at a time, in deep, hot
oil. Fry till delicately golden. Mix the soya sauce, pineapple, green pepper, carrots, water, vinegar, sugar,
and molasses and cook slowly, stirring well. Let boil
3 minutes. Mix the cornstarch and pineapple juice.

87

Stir into the mixture and cook till thickened. Add the chicken, mix, and serve. 4 servings.

CRISP SKIN
CHICKEN

> 5-pound roasting chicken
> 2 cups hot water
> ½ cup honey
> ¼ cup vinegar
> 1 tablespoon molasses
> ½ cup soya sauce
> 2 tablespoons gin
> 2 tablespoons flour
> 3 teaspoons salt
> ½ cup cooking oil
> Thin slices fresh bread
> Young scallions, cut in 1½-inch pieces
> Mustard Sauce
> Plum Sauce
> Celery salt

Draw and wash chicken. Par-cook the chicken in the hot water 45 minutes. Drain, rinse under cold water. Wipe dry. Mix the honey, vinegar, molasses, soya sauce, and gin, and brush over the chicken. Let dry. Brush over again with the mixture. Sprinkle with flour and salt and let dry, then fry in very hot oil. The chicken should brown in 2 or 3 minutes.

88

Remove the chicken, drain it, and cut off the skin. Serve the crisp, delicious skin as an appetizer with the chicken; fold it in a thin slice of bread with a piece of scallion, and Mustard and Plum Sauces. Cut the chicken and serve it. Serve little dishes of celery salt with it so each piece may be dipped in the salt. 4 or more servings.

CHICKEN
WITH ALMONDS

3 tablespoons cooking oil
1 teaspoon salt
2 cups diced raw chicken, dark or white meat, or both
2 tablespoons soya sauce
1 cup fresh peas or sliced string beans
1 cup diced celery heart
½ cup canned button mushrooms
1 cup boiling water
1 tablespoon cornstarch
¼ cup cold water
½ cup toasted almonds

Heat the oil and salt in a large, heavy frying pan; add chicken and cook till almost done—about 3 minutes. Add the soya sauce; mix. Add vegetables and boiling water. Stir and mix. Cover the pot; cook till steaming. Stir and cook 5 or 7 minutes, or till chicken and vegetables are done. Mix cornstarch and cold water; add to the mixture; cook and stir till thickened. Add almonds; mix. Serve. 4 servings.

CUBED CHICKEN
WITH
MUSHROOMS

> 3 cups cubed raw chicken
> 2 teaspoons salt
> 3 tablespoons cooking oil
> 2 tablespoons soya sauce
> 1 cup green peas
> ½ cup sliced canned water chestnuts, optional
> 1 cup sliced celery
> 1½ teaspoons sugar
> ¼ teaspoon pepper
> 1½ cups stock or hot water
> 2 cups sliced fresh or canned button mushrooms
> 2 teaspoons cornstarch
> ¼ cup cold water

Season the chicken with 1 teaspoon salt. Heat the oil in a large, heavy frying pan and sauté the chicken in it till light golden. Dash 1 tablespoon soya sauce over the chicken; stir; mix. Add the peas, water chestnuts, celery, 1 teaspoon salt, sugar, pepper, and stock or hot water. Stir. Cover the pot. Bring to boiling point; stir; mix. Cover and let cook 4 minutes. Add the mushrooms Cover and let cook 3 or 4 minutes longer. Mix the remaining tablespoon of soya sauce with the cornstarch in cold water. Stir into the chicken mixture till the sauce is thickened. Serve hot with rice. 4 to 6 servings.

CHINESE CREAMED CHICKEN

2 eggs
4 tablespoons flour or cornstarch
1 young hen
4 or 5 tablespoons cooking oil
3 cups milk or 1 large can
    condensed milk
1 cup water
1 teaspoon salt
½ teaspoon pepper
1 cup sliced fresh or button
    mushrooms, optional

Draw and wash chicken; cut in serving pieces. Beat eggs slightly; mix with flour and just enough water to make a thin batter. Dip the chicken in the batter. Heat the oil, sauté the chicken, cooking till well browned on all sides. Pour in milk and water to barely cover the chicken; add salt and pepper. Bring to boiling. Cover and cook very slowly 30 to 45 minutes. Add mushrooms and continue cooking 5 to 10 minutes longer. Serve hot. 4 servings.

POT ROAST CHICKEN WITH MUSHROOMS

3 to 4-pound young chicken
1 teaspoon salt
5 tablespoons cooking oil
¼ cup soya sauce
2 tablespoons gin
1 teaspoon sugar
2 cups boiling water
1 pound fresh mushrooms, cut in halves
1 teaspoon salt
½ teaspoon pepper
2 tablespoons cornstarch
¼ cup hot water or stock
4 or 5 slender scallions, cut in 1-inch lengths

Leave the cleaned chicken whole. Rinse it; wipe dry. Heat salt and oil in a deep, heavy aluminum pot; brown the chicken evenly on all sides. Use moderate heat. Turn it frequently. Mix the soya sauce, gin, and sugar, and pour over the chicken. Cover and let stand on very low heat 3 to 5 minutes; the steam cooks the flavor into the chicken. Then add the boiling water, scatter the mushrooms over the chicken, sprinkle all with salt and pepper. Cover the pot again, turn the heat up, and when boiling lower the heat and cook 30 minutes.

Remove pot from heat; take chicken out and let it cool a little, then remove the bones: break the wing, pull it off, and pull out the bone; break off the legs, pull out bones. Cut meat off breast. Arrange the chicken meat on a hot platter. Mix cornstarch and water or stock. Stir into the pot. Cook till thickened. Add scallions, mix, and pour over the chicken. Serve at once. 4 to 6 servings.

SMOOTH CHICKEN

> 1 tender young chicken
> 6 tablespoons cornstarch or flour
> ½ cup cold water
> 2 egg whites
> 2 quarts boiling water
> 2 cups fresh or quick-frozen peas
> ½ cup fresh mushrooms, cut in halves
> 1 teaspoon salt
> ½ teaspoon pepper
> 1 tablespoon soya sauce

Remove skin from the chicken; cut all meat off in serving-size pieces. Mix 4 tablespoons cornstarch with ¼ cup cold water and slightly beaten egg whites. Dip the chicken pieces in this. Let stand a few minutes. Have 2 quarts of water boiling rapidly. Drop the chicken into it, a piece at a time, but keep the water boiling. Place these parboiled pieces in a colander, rinse with cold water, drain.

Cook the peas and mushrooms together in 1½ cups boiling water about 3 minutes after it begins to boil. Add the chicken, salt, and pepper. Cover the pot and let cook and steam 10 to 15 minutes longer. Mix the remaining tablespoons cornstarch with ¼ cup cold water and stir into the pan. Stir and cook till thickened. Add soya sauce, mix, and serve. 4 to 6 servings.

STEAMED CHICKEN

4-pound plump chicken
2 teaspoons salt
1 teaspoon pepper
2 tablespoons soya sauce
2 tablespoons sherry
2 tablespoons cooking oil or chicken fat
1 cup sliced fresh or dried mushrooms (if latter, soaked then squeezed dry)
3 teaspoons cornstarch

Draw and wash chicken. Cut meat from bones; spread it in a shallow casserole or on a platter. Mix salt, pepper, soya sauce, sherry, oil or fat, and mushrooms, and spread over chicken. Sprinkle the cornstarch over all. Mix well. Set the dish on a high rack in a deep kettle; add boiling water to the kettle up to within 1 inch of the rack. Cover kettle tightly. Bring water to boiling point. Steam 20 to 30 minutes. 4 or 5 servings.

> *Variation: In place of mushrooms add ½ cup shredded boiled or baked ham to the platter, pour the sauce over, and steam as described.*

LEFTOVER ROAST CHICKEN

1 cup or more diced cooked chicken

2 cups raw string beans, sliced crosswise

½ cup diced canned water chestnuts, optional

½ cup diced onion, optional

1 cup boiling water or chicken stock

1 tablespoon soya sauce

½ teaspoon sugar

½ teaspoon salt

2½ teaspoons cornstarch

¼ cup cold water

95

Add the chicken, string beans, chestnuts (if used), and onion to the boiling water or stock. Bring to boiling point; cook 5 minutes. Stir the soya sauce, sugar, and salt into the sauce. Mix the cornstarch and cold water and stir in. Cook till thickened. Serve at once. 4 servings.

Note: To vary this add ½ cup mushrooms and ½ to 1 cup chopped celery and omit onion.

ROAST GOOSE CHINESE STYLE

7 to 8-pound young goose
½ garlic clove
1 teaspoon cooking oil
½ onion, chopped
¼ cup chopped celery
½ teaspoon powdered cinnamon
1 or 2 anise seeds
¾ cup soya sauce
1 tablespoon sugar
Boiling water
½ cup salt
½ cup honey
¼ cup vinegar
1 tablespoon molasses or soya sauce
Boiling water

Draw, wash, and drain the goose; wipe dry inside and

out. Mash the garlic in a hot pan with the oil and continue to heat till the garlic is black, then discard the garlic. Add the onion, stir, and cook 2 minutes; add the celery, stir, and mix; sprinkle with cinnamon and anise seeds; add soya sauce and sugar and stir. Add 2 cups boiling water, mix, bring to boiling, and turn off the heat.

Tie the goose neck with string so the sauce will not bubble out. Pour the sauce inside the bird, sew up vent, or fasten with small skewers. Rub salt over the whole bird. Lay it on a greased rack, breast up, in an open roasting pan; place uncovered in a hot oven, 400° F., 20 minutes to brown; lower the heat to 375° F., and continue roasting 2½ to 3 hours (allow 20 to 25 minutes per pound).

Add 2 cups boiling water to the honey, the vinegar, and molasses or soya sauce. Mix and brush over the bird after the first 30 minutes of roasting. Then repeat every 20 minutes. Reduce heat to 300° F. for the last half hour of cooking. Let cool slightly, remove string or skewers. Drain contents out and serve with the goose as a sauce or make a gravy by thickening it with a little cornstarch. 8 to 10 servings.

ROAST DUCK CHINESE STYLE Follow recipe for Roast Goose Chinese Style. Use the honey-and-water basting twice on the roasting duck.

Use 4 to 6-pound duck; allow 25 to 35 minutes per pound roasting time. 4 to 6 servings.

FIVE SAVORIES
SQUAB

4 squabs
3 cups soya sauce
¾ cup sugar
1 tablespoon powdered
  cinnamon
1 or 2 anise seeds
3 cups water
Oil for deep frying
2 or 3 young scallions, chopped
  green and white
Celery salt

Draw and rinse squabs; drain. In a deep, narrow kettle
mix the soya sauce, sugar, cinnamon, anise seeds, and
water. When boiling, add the squabs. Reduce heat at
once, then slowly let the heat come up to just below
the simmering point. Let stand 30 minutes. Drain the
squabs; fry in deep hot oil till brown. Drain. Sprinkle
with chopped scallions. Serve whole or cut in halves.
Provide a little dish of celery salt for each person, in
which the pieces may be dipped. 4 or more servings.

牧童晚歸

Meat Recipes

牧童晚歸

BEEF
AND
BROCCOLI

> 1½ pounds broccoli
> ½ pound beef, cut in slices ¼ inch thick and about 1½ inches square
> 4 tablespoons cooking oil
> 1 small sliver garlic, mashed
> 1 teaspoon sugar
> 1 teaspoon salt
> 2 tablespoons soya sauce
> 2 teaspoons rice wine or gin
> ¾ cup water
> 2 tablespoons cornstarch
> ¼ cup water

Wash broccoli; slice stalks in thin slantwise pieces about 1½ inches long. Sauté the beef in the hot oil with the garlic, sugar, salt, soya sauce, and rice wine or gin.

Cook 2 or 3 minutes. Remove meat. Add broccoli and water to pan. Cover; let come to boiling; stir. Cover and cook 2 or 3 minutes. Add the meat. Mix the cornstarch and water; stir. Pour over the mixture. Cook 2 or 3 minutes, or till the sauce is thickened. Serve hot. 4 servings.

BEEF AND RICE

                    3 or 4 cups freshly cooked hot
                      rice (see rice recipe)
                    3 tablespoons cooking oil
                    1 small sliver garlic
                    ½ teaspoon salt
                    ¼ teaspoon pepper
                    1 pound beef, ground
                    3 tablespoons soya sauce
                    1 cup boiling water
                    3 scallions, cut in 1½-inch pieces
                    ½ cup sliced fresh or canned
                      mushrooms, optional
                    2 teaspoons cornstarch
                    4 tablespoons cold water
                    4 eggs

Have a 2-quart casserole ready, or 4 individual casseroles. As soon as the rice is cooked, heat oil; mash garlic into the hot oil; add salt and pepper; sauté the

102

beef in it 3 or 4 minutes. Add soya sauce, boiling water, scallions, and mushrooms. Let come to boiling point. Cook and stir 2 or 3 minutes. Mix cornstarch and water; stir into the pan and cook till the sauce is thickened. Place the hot rice in one large casserole or in 4 individual casseroles. Pour the sauce over the rice. Use a spoon to make a depression in the center of the rice. (Or four depressions in the large casserole.) Break an egg into each depression. Cover the dish at once. The eggs cook in the hot rice and sauce. 4 servings.

VARIATION

CURRIED BEEF AND RICE   Add 1 or 2 tablespoons of curry powder to the hot pan in which the meat is cooked, then follow recipe directions.

BEEF CURRY
WITH ONIONS

4 tablespoons curry powder
½ clove garlic
2 tablespoons cooking oil
1 teaspoon salt
¼ teaspoon pepper
1 thin slice green ginger root,
    mashed, optional
2 pounds beef, cut in small cubes

4 small onions, cut in slender
strips
3 tablespoons soya sauce
1 cup beef or chicken bouillon,
or hot water
2 tablespoons cornstarch
¼ cup cold water

Stir the curry powder in the center of a large, heavy
frying pan. When very hot, add the garlic, mash it,
then stir in the oil, a little at a time; add the salt,
pepper, and ginger, if used. Mix well. Add the meat,
stirring well; add the onions; stir and cook till the
onions are tender. Add the soya sauce and bouillon or
hot water. Cover the pan, bring to boiling point and
cook 3 minutes. Mix cornstarch and water; stir into the
meat mixture and cook till sauce is thickened. Serve
hot. 6 servings.

**BEEF
WITH BEAN
SPROUTS**

1 pound flank steak
4 tablespoons cooking oil
½ garlic clove, mashed
1 teaspoon salt
½ teaspoon pepper
1 teaspoon mashed green ginger
root, optional

4 tablespoons soya sauce
½ teaspoon sugar
2 cups canned or fresh bean
    sprouts
3 tablespoons cornstarch
¼ cup cold water
2 or 3 young scallions, cut in
    1½-inch pieces

Slice the steak as thin as possible in short crosswise pieces. Heat oil, garlic, salt, pepper, and ginger root (if used) together. Cook beef in this till almost done. Cover the pan and let cook 1 or 2 minutes. If fresh bean sprouts are used, remove the beef, bring to boiling and cook the sprouts 3 minutes. Add the meat again. Stir. Mix cornstarch and cold water, pour over the mixture; stir and cook till sauce is thickened. Sprinkle with scallions and serve. 4 servings.

BEEF WITH TOMATOES AND PEPPERS   See recipe for Beef with Bean Sprouts. Add 2 tomatoes cut in quarters or sixths and 2 green peppers cut in 1½-inch pieces when the bean sprouts are added. Cook as directed. 4 to 6 servings.

Note: This may be served over cooked noodles or rice.

BEEF
WITH
MUSHROOMS

1 pound fresh mushrooms, or
  ½ pound dried mushrooms
2 cups beef bouillon, chicken
  stock, or hot water
½ teaspoon salt
1½ pounds sliced fresh beef or
  the same amount leftover
  roast beef with fat trimmed off
2 tablespoons cooking oil
1 small sliver garlic
½ teaspoon pepper
1 small onion, diced
2 tablespoons sherry
1 tablespoon soya sauce
1 tablespoon cornstarch
¼ cup cold water

If dried mushrooms are used, wash them, drain, cover
with cold water, and let soak 1 hour. Drain, remove
stems, and cut mushrooms in halves. Then cook (fresh
or dried) mushrooms in the chicken stock or hot
water, with salt, 10 minutes. Sauté the beef in the oil
with the garlic, pepper, and onion, and cook 1 minute;
add sherry and soya sauce. Add all to the mushrooms;
mix. Let cook 1 or 2 minutes. Mix cornstarch and cold
water, stir into the mushroom mixture till sauce is
thickened. Serve hot. 4 or more servings.

MINCED STRING BEANS WITH BEEF

2 tablespoons cooking oil
1 or 2 small onions, diced
1 teaspoon salt
½ teaspoon pepper
1 small sliver garlic
½ pound beef, diced fine
2 tablespoons soya sauce
1 pound young green string
   beans, diced fine
1 cup hot water or stock
1 tablespoon cornstarch, optional
¼ cup cold water

Heat oil; cook onions 1 or 2 minutes; add seasonings and garlic; cook 1 minute; add meat, stir and cook 1 or 2 minutes. Remove meat, then add soya sauce, beans, and water; mix and stir. Cover the pan; cook on low heat till beans are tender—10 to 15 minutes. Add meat again. If thickening is desired, mix the cornstarch and cold water; stir into the mixture and cook till the sauce is thickened. 2 to 4 servings.

VARIATION

STRING BEANS AND BEEF, CHINESE STYLE   Cut the beef in very thin, small pieces, and cut the beans in 1½-inch lengths. Cook as described in recipe above.

107

BEEF
WITH GINGER

½ cup thin slices fresh ginger
    root
6 tablespoons salt
1 pound beef, sliced very thin
6 tablespoons cooking oil
½ clove garlic, mashed
3 tablespoons soya sauce
2 teaspoons sherry
2 teaspoons sugar
¼ teaspoon pepper
2 tablespoons cornstarch
¼ cup cold water

Mix the ginger and salt; stir. Let stand 15 minutes, then rinse the ginger well with cold water to draw out the hotness. Drain. Heat the oil in a heavy frying pan; add the garlic and ginger; stir. Add beef and cook 3 to 5 minutes. Add soya sauce, sherry, sugar, and pepper. Stir and cook till the meat is nearly done. Mix cornstarch and water; stir into the meat and cook till sauce is thickened. Serve hot. 4 servings.

Note: This dish is best in wintertime. It is sometimes served on top of hot rice.

FIVE-FLAVOR
BEEF

> 4-pound piece of beef brisket or
>   chuck, very small amount of
>   fat left on
> 4 tablespoons cooking oil
> 2 cups soya sauce
> 2 cups water
> 1-inch piece stick cinnamon
> 1 or 2 anise seeds
> ½ cup sugar
> 1 tablespoon salt
> 1 cup sherry

Use a Dutch oven or heavy aluminum pot. Sear the meat in it in the oil till browned on all sides. Mix the remaining ingredients except the sherry and pour over the meat. Cover the pot and cook on low heat 2 to 3 hours, or till tender. Stir sauce and spoon it over the meat from time to time. Add the sherry to the sauce for the last hour of cooking.

When the meat is done, stir sauce, increase heat, and cook it down to a thickened gravy, till practically all is absorbed and cooked into the meat. Serve hot. Or chill and slice very thin. This will keep in refrigerator for several days and is used like ham for sandwiches or cold cuts. 8 to 12 servings.

BEST FLAVOR
CUBED BEEF

1 pound beef, cut in large cubes
3 tablespoons cooking oil
1 sliver garlic, mashed
1 teaspoon salt
4 tablespoons soya sauce
½ cup Oyster Sauce, bought, or
   see recipe
2 teaspoons sugar
2 teaspoons rice wine or gin
2 cups boiling water
2 or 3 young scallions, chopped
   green and white, or 2 or 3
   fresh or canned mushrooms,
   sliced

Sauté the beef in the hot oil with garlic and salt. When lightly cooked on all sides, mix soya sauce, Oyster Sauce, sugar, wine or gin. Pour over the meat. Stir; cover. Add boiling water. Cook slowly 25 minutes, till sauce is cooked down. Add scallions or mushrooms, stir 2 minutes, and serve. 4 servings.

CHINESE
BEEF STEW

2-pound piece stewing beef
3 tablespoons cooking oil
1 cup soya sauce
3 cups water

1-inch piece stick cinnamon
1 or 2 anise seeds
1 tablespoon salt
1 tablespoon sugar
¾ cup sherry
1 pound celery, cut in 1-inch pieces
4 young white turnips, scraped and cut in quarters

Sauté the beef in the oil till golden on all sides. Mix soya sauce, water, cinnamon, anise seeds, salt, sugar, and sherry and pour over the beef. Cover, bring to boiling point; lower heat and cook 45 minutes on just enough heat to bring to boiling point. Add celery and turnips. Add additional hot water if needed. Cover the pot and continue cooking 20 minutes, or till meat and vegetables are done. 6 servings.

SLICED BEEF
WITH CABBAGE

1 pound beef, sliced thin and cut
in strips 1½ inches square and
¼-inch thick
3 tablespoons oil
1 small sliver garlic, mashed
1 teaspoon salt
½ teaspoon pepper
1 small, thin slice green ginger
root or ½ teaspoon powdered
ginger, optional
1 ½-pound head cabbage, cut in
1½-inch cubes
1 teaspoon sugar
2 tablespoons soya sauce
1 tablespoon cornstarch
¼ cup cold water

Sauté the beef in the hot oil with the garlic; add salt,
pepper, and ginger. Stir and cook 2 or 3 minutes.
When nearly done, remove meat. Add cabbage, sprinkle with sugar. Turn heat low, cook and stir 2 minutes;
add meat again and soya sauce. Mix, turn heat high
again, and stir and cook 2 minutes. Mix cornstarch and
cold water and stir into the pan. Cook and stir till
sauce is thickened. Serve hot. 2 to 4 servings.

STEAMED BEEF WITH DRIED MUSHROOMS

1 pound beef, sliced thin
½ cup dried washed mushrooms,
    soaked ½ hour, squeezed dry
1 teaspoon salt
¼ teaspoon pepper
3 tablespoons soya sauce
2 tablespoons sherry
½ teaspoon sugar
2 tablespoons cooking oil or
    chicken fat
½ teaspoon grated lemon peel
1 tablespoon cornstarch
¼ cup cold water

Season the meat with salt and pepper and place in a shallow casserole or on a platter. Cover with mushrooms. Mix all ingredients except cornstarch and cold water and pour over the beef. Set the dish on a rack in a kettle. Pour boiling water in the kettle up to within 1 inch of the rack. Cover kettle tightly; bring water to boiling point. Steam 20 to 25 minutes, or till meat is done. Add cornstarch and water mixed; stir until same is thickened. 4 servings.

DICED BEEF AND PEAS

1 pound fresh, tender young
  baby peas or frozen peas
1 cup diced raw beef
3 tablespoons cooking oil
1 small sliver garlic, mashed
2 teaspoons salt
½ teaspoon pepper
½ cup sliced fresh or canned
  button mushrooms
¾ cup hot water or stock
2 tablespoons soya sauce
2 tablespoons cornstarch
¼ cup cold water

Use the smallest, youngest peas available. Sauté the beef in the hot oil with the garlic, salt, and pepper. When the meat is lightly cooked, remove it, add the peas, mushrooms and hot water or stock. Stir. Cover the pan, bring to boiling point and let cook 5 to 8 minutes. Add the beef again. Mix the soya sauce, cornstarch, and water, stir into the pan, and cook and stir till the sauce is thickened. Serve hot. 4 to 6 servings.

MEAT DISHES WITH PORK

PORK AND BROCCOLI See Beef and Broccoli. Use sliced fresh pork shoulder in place of beef and follow

directions. Cook the pork thoroughly and do not remove pork before adding broccoli.

PORK
WITH
STRING BEANS

1 pound young green string
    beans
¾ pound ground pork shoulder
2 tablespoons cooking oil
1 small piece garlic, mashed
2 tablespoons soya sauce
½ teaspoon salt
1 onion, diced, or ½ cup canned
    water chestnuts, drained and
    chopped
1½ cups boiling water
1 tablespoon cornstarch
¼ cup cold water
½ head green lettuce, chopped

Wash the beans, cut crosswise in very small pieces.
Sauté the meat in the hot oil with the garlic. Stir and
cook till browned. Add soya sauce, salt, onion or water
chestnuts; cook 1 or 2 minutes; stir. Add the beans and
boiling water; mix. Cover the pan, bring to boiling
point, and cook 2 or 3 minutes; stir again. Cover and
cook 2 minutes. Mix cornstarch and cold water; stir

into the meat and beans. Stir and cook till sauce is thickened.

Place the chopped lettuce in a warm serving dish. Pour the meat mixture over it. Serve at once. 4 servings.

BAKED PORK
WITH
CELERY CABBAGE

3 or 4-pound piece pork
   shoulder, cut 2 inches thick
1½ teaspoons salt
1 teaspoon pepper
4 tablespoons soya sauce
1 tablespoon sugar
1 small sliver garlic, mashed
1 head Chinese celery cabbage

Leave pork in one piece. Mix salt, pepper, soya sauce, sugar, and spread over it. Let stand with sauce on it in refrigerator 1 hour. Bake, uncovered, in a moderate oven (350° F.) 1 hour, or till meat is almost tender. Lift meat out, drain off fat. Wash cabbage and cut the head in half lengthwise. Place the cabbage in the baking pan, cut side up. Lay the pork on the cabbage, cover the pan; continue to bake 45 minutes longer. Place on a hot serving dish, the cabbage first and the meat on top. 6 or more servings.

SWEET
AND PUNGENT
PORK

1 pound pork shoulder, cut in
cubes
Oil for deep frying
1 cup canned pineapple cubes
1 green pepper, cut diagonally in
about 1-inch wide pieces
½ cup vinegar
¼ cup brown sugar
1 cup water
1 tablespoon molasses
1 tomato, cut in 4 to 6 pieces
2 tablespoons cornstarch

BATTER

1 egg
½ cup flour
½ teaspoon salt
3 or 4 tablespoons water

Beat the egg; mix flour, salt, and water with it to form
a thin batter. Pour over pork, mix to coat the pieces,
then fry them, piece by piece, in deep, hot oil till
browned. Drain.

Mix pineapple, green pepper, vinegar, sugar, ¾ cup
water, and molasses. Stir until it boils; add tomato.
Mix cornstarch with remaining ¼ cup water and stir
into the sauce. Cook till thickened. Add pork, stir to
mix well, and serve at once. 4 servings.

STEAMED PORK WITH CHINESE CHEESE

1 pound pork shoulder, cut in
very thin slices
2 cubes (tablespoons) Chinese
Cheese (Foo Yee)
1½ teaspoons cornstarch
3 tablespoons cold water
1 teaspoon soya sauce

Lay the pork slices in a shallow casserole or on a platter. Mix other ingredients smoothly together, mix well into meat. Set the dish on a rack in a pan. Pour boiling water in the pan to within 1 inch of the rack. Cover and bring to boiling, and steam 30 to 40 minutes. 4 servings.

PORK WITH FRESH MUSHROOMS

½ pound fresh mushrooms
1 pound pork shoulder, cut in
very thin 1½-inch squares
2 tablespoons cooking oil
½ teaspoon salt
2 tablespoons soya sauce

1 cup boiling water
1 tablespoon cornstarch
¼ cup cold water

Wash mushrooms, remove stems; cut caps in 2 or 3 pieces. Sauté pork in hot oil and salt till golden; add soya sauce and boiling water; mix. Cover the pan and let boil 5 minutes. Add mushrooms; mix; cook 2 or 3 minutes. Mix cornstarch with cold water. Stir into the mushroom mixture and cook till sauce is thickened. Serve hot. 2 to 4 servings.

> *Note: Mushroom stems may be sliced and boiled or sautéed and used in various dishes which call for mushrooms.*

CURRIED PORK AND CELERY

1½ pounds pork shoulder, cut in large cubes
3 tablespoons cooking oil
2 teaspoons salt
3 or 4 tablespoons curry powder
1½ cups boiling water
¾ pound celery, cut in 1-inch lengths (use large outside stalks)

Sauté the pork in the oil till well browned; season with

salt. Push meat to one side of the pan, stir the curry powder into the hot oil, and blend and cook 1 or 2 minutes, then mix with the meat. Add the boiling water; cover; bring to boiling point, and let cook slowly 20 minutes. Add celery; mix. Cover the pan again, bring to boiling point, and cook 10 minutes. Stir a few times during cooking. 4 servings.

紫蟹芙蓉

Egg Recipes

EGGS
AND
SCALLOPS SAUTÉ

2 cups small fresh scallops
5 tablespoons cooking oil
1 teaspoon salt
¼ teaspoon pepper
½ cup chopped onions
1 tablespoon soya sauce
4 eggs
½ cup chopped scallions, green
and white

If scallops are large, cut in small pieces. Heat oil; sprinkle salt and pepper into the hot oil. Add the onions and cook till clear. Add the scallops. Stir and cook, uncovered, on low heat. Dash soya sauce over them. Beat the eggs lightly, mix with scallions; pour

over the scallops and cook only till the eggs are set.
Serve at once. 4 servings.

EGGS AND SHRIMP SAUTÉ   Use 2 cups small cooked
or canned shrimp in place of scallops in above recipe.

**EGGS AND
CRAB MEAT
SAUTÉ**

> 1 cup cooked or canned crab
>   meat
> 2 tablespoons cooking oil or
>   chicken fat
> 1 cup fresh or canned bean
>   sprouts, rinsed and drained
> 1½ teaspoons salt
> ½ teaspoon pepper
> 6 eggs
> 2 or 3 young scallions, chopped
>   green and white

Look over crab meat and remove any cartilage. Heat
the oil or fat in a frying pan; sauté the crab meat about
1 minute; add bean sprouts. Sprinkle with salt and
pepper, mix, and cook 1 minute. Beat eggs lightly and
stir carefully into mixture. Cook on low heat; stir once

or twice, do not scramble. Scatter scallions over the top. Serve as soon as eggs are set. 4 servings.

EGGS AND BEAN SPROUTS SAUTÉ Omit sea food from above recipe; add 1 extra cup bean sprouts, ¼ cup chopped onion, and ¼ cup chopped green pepper.

EGG FOO YOUNG

1 cup leftover chopped cooked ham or roast pork
½ cup chopped onion
1 cup fresh or canned bean sprouts, rinsed and drained
3 tablespoons chopped scallions
1 tablespoon soya sauce
1 teaspoon salt
3 eggs
Oil for deep frying

SAUCE

1½ cups chicken stock
1 teaspoon molasses
1 teaspoon soya sauce
1 teaspoon cornstarch mixed with
2 tablespoons cold water

Place meat, onion, sprouts, scallions, soya sauce, and salt in a bowl and mix well together. Break eggs and

125

stir lightly into the mixture. With deep-bowl ladle spoon out the mixture and lower into the hot oil; tip the ladle at once to release the omelets. Let them fry till they rise to the top. Turn them over (like doughnuts) and let the other side brown. Lift out at once with a large strainer spoon. Put on a hot dish. Serve plain, dashed with soya sauce. 4 servings.

Heat stock, molasses, soya sauce, cornstarch, and water. Stir until smooth. Let come to boiling point and cook only till thickened. Spoon a little over the Egg Foo Young.

FOO YOUNG VARIATIONS

CHICKEN FOO YOUNG Use chopped cooked chicken in place of ham or pork.

CRAB MEAT FOO YOUNG Use fresh, quick-frozen, or canned crab meat in place of ham or pork.

SHRIMP FOO YOUNG Use cooked or canned shrimp in place of ham or pork.

VEGETABLE FOO YOUNG Use 2 cups chopped green pepper, celery, onion, and canned bean sprouts combined; omit meat, shrimp, or chicken; add 1 extra teaspoon salt.

126

LOBSTER FOO YOUNG Use cooked or canned lobster meat in place of ham or pork.

SUBGUM FOO YOUNG To any of the above recipes add 1 cup diced mushrooms, ½ cup diced string beans, ½ cup diced fresh or canned bamboo shoots. Mix and cook as described. 4 servings.

> *Note: Egg Foo Young may be pan-fried in a very little oil. Grease a hot skillet well with cooking oil or chicken fat. Fry the spoonfuls of egg mixture till brown on both sides.*

**STEAMED EGGS
AND SHRIMP**

¼ pound pork shoulder, ground
½ pound fresh shrimp
¼ cup chopped scallions, green and white
1½ teaspoons salt
1 teaspoon grated lemon peel
6 eggs
½ cup water
Soya sauce

Shell and clean shrimp. Grind meat and shrimp to-

127

gether; add scallions, salt, and lemon peel, and put
through the grinder two more times. Beat and pound
till smooth. Beat eggs, slowly adding the water to
them. Mix thoroughly and add to meat mixture.
Spread on a platter and set it on the rack in a pan.
Pour boiling water into the pan up to within 1 inch of
the rack. Cover the pan. Bring to boiling point. Cook
20 to 30 minutes, or till meat is cooked. Dash with
soya sauce. 4 servings.

STEAMED EGGS
AND FISH
FRIDAY FISH

> 1 large flounder cleaned and
>   filleted, or 1 pound fish fillets
> 4 eggs
> ½ cup water
> 1 teaspoon salt
> 1 tablespoon lemon peel, cut in
>   thin threads
> ½ teaspoon pepper
> 1 or 2 tablespoons cooking oil or
>   chicken fat
> 2 or 3 young scallions, chopped
>   green and white
> Soya sauce

Mash or grind fish fillets; beat eggs with water; add to

fish with salt, pepper, fat, and lemon peel. Spread on a platter; set it on a rack in a pan. Pour boiling water into the pan up to within 1 inch of the rack. Cover the pan. Bring the water to boiling point. Let steam 20 to 30 minutes, till eggs and fish are cooked. Sprinkle with scallions, dash with soya sauce, and serve. 4 servings.

> *Variation: Use any delicate fish available; vary seasoning by adding a very little spice, such as cinnamon or ginger, to the mixture.*

祝
壽

Chow Mein

祝
壽

CHICKEN CHOW MEIN

4 tablespoons cooking oil or
  chicken fat
3 teaspoons salt
¼ teaspoon pepper
2 cups sliced Chinese cabbage
3 cups shredded celery
2 cups canned bean sprouts,
  optional
2 teaspoons sugar
2 cups stock or water
4 tablespoons soya sauce
2½ tablespoons cornstarch
¼ cup cold water
2 cups sliced cooked chicken, cut
  in thin slivers or shredded
  fresh chicken
1 8-ounce package thin noodles,
  fried (see recipe)
2 hard-cooked eggs, chopped or
  sliced, optional

133

Heat oil, salt, and pepper in a deep hot skillet; add all the vegetables, the bean sprouts last; sprinkle the sugar over them; stir. Add the stock or water; mix well. Cover the pan. Cook till boiling point, then turn the mixture over. Cover and let cook till boiling point, about 10 minutes in all. Stir, add the soya mixed with cornstarch and water; stir slowly while the mixture thickens. Add the chicken. Stir till all is thickened and smooth.

Place fried noodles on a large platter or in 4 individual dishes. Pour the mixture over the noodles. Top with the sliced or chopped eggs. 4 servings.

HOW TO FRY NOODLES   Buy the thinnest egg noodles available. Drop into boiling water. Remove at once. Drain. Spread in a large colander, place over pan of boiling water, and steam 20 minutes. Drain.

Pan-fry in hot oil; or drop in deep, hot oil and fry till crisp. Drain and use as directed.

> *Note: Chinese fried noodles may be bought in vacuum-packed tins; they may be reheated to crispness in a hot oven, or follow directions on the can.*

CHOW MEIN VARIATIONS

SHRIMP CHOW MEIN   Use 2 cups diced cooked or canned shrimp in place of chicken.

CHOW MEIN WITH ALMONDS Add ½ cup sliced toasted almonds as topping in place of the hard-cooked egg.

CHOW MEIN WITH MUSHROOMS Add 1½ cups thinly sliced fresh or canned mushrooms to the vegetables and cook as directed.

CHOW MEIN WITH PINEAPPLE Add 1 or 1½ cups diced or shredded pineapple when adding the soya sauce and cornstarch. Stir and cook 3 or 4 minutes to thicken.

BEEF OR PORK CHOW MEIN Use 2 cups roast beef or pork, cut in thin slivers, in place of chicken.

SUBGUM CHOW MEIN Subgum means "10 different varieties of beauty." The subgum chow mein means an elaboration of the usual chow mein to include 10 different vegetables, such as canned water chestnuts, canned bamboo shoots, celery, celery cabbage, mushrooms, green pepper, string beans, onions, almonds, noodles, and the chicken, meat, or shrimp, and the sauce. Prepare like Chow Mein.

CANTONESE STYLE SUBGUM CHOW MEIN means with crisp noodles, pan-fried, or deep-fat fried noodles.

BEEF
AND TOMATO
LO MEIN

8-ounce package fine noodles
3 teaspoons salt
Boiling water
3 tablespoons cooking oil
½ garlic clove, mashed
½ teaspoon pepper
1 pound chopped steak or hamburger
2 tomatoes, cut in quarters or in sixths
1 tablespoon sugar
1 cup boiling water or stock
1 teaspoon cornstarch
¼ cup cold water
3 or 4 young scallions, cut in 1-inch lengths

Boil noodles in salted water as directed on the package, 8 to 10 minutes; drain in a colander, rinse under running cold water, and drain again.

Heat the oil with the garlic, remaining 1 teaspoon salt, and the pepper in a large, heavy skillet. Add the meat and cook till nearly done. Add the tomatoes, sugar, and water or stock; stir and mix. Cook to boiling point. Add cornstarch mixed with cold water. Stir and cook till the sauce is thickened. Add noodles. Stir only till noodles are hot. Serve, garnished with scallions. 4 servings.

CHICKEN LO MEIN Use Chicken Chow Mein recipe, but first sauté the chicken in the 4 tablespoons oil; add the seasonings and vegetables as directed; cover and let steam. Uncover, turn the mixture, cover, and let cook a few minutes still steaming. Add the soya sauce and cornstarch as directed. Stir till thickened slightly, then add boiled and drained noodles. Stir to heat the noodles through. Sprinkle finely chopped scallions over the top. Serve at once. 4 servings.

黄花绿身

Chop Suey

PORK
CHOP SUEY

3 tablespoons cooking oil
2 teaspoons salt
½ teaspoon pepper
1 pound pork shoulder, cut in
    small cubes
2½ tablespoons soya sauce
3 cups celery, cut in 1-inch
    lengths
2 big onions, each cut in 6 pieces
1 tablespoon molasses
2 cups boiling water or stock
1 can or 2 cups fresh bean
    sprouts, rinsed and drained
3 tablespoons cornstarch
¼ cup cold water

Have ready a large, heavy skillet or pot. Heat the oil,
salt, and pepper together. Add pork; sear. Stir 5 or 8

minutes. Add soya sauce; mix. Add celery and onions; stir and cook 3 or 4 minutes. Mix molasses and boiling water or stock and pour over the mixture; stir. Cover and cook over low heat 20 to 30 minutes. Add bean sprouts; stir and cook 2 or 3 minutes. Mix cornstarch with cold water; stir into the Chop Suey; mix and cook till the sauce is thickened. Serve with hot rice. 4 to 6 servings.

CHOP SUEY VARIATIONS

SHRIMP CHOP SUEY Substitute 2 cups chopped cooked or canned shrimp in place of beef in the Beef Chop Suey recipe.

BEEF CHOP SUEY Substitute beef for pork in Pork Chop Suey. Cook beef in the hot oil 3 or 4 minutes. Remove the meat. Add celery and onions to oil, soya sauce, molasses, and boiling water or stock; stir and cook 10 minutes. Add sprouts; stir and cook 2 or 3 minutes. Add beef. Mix cornstarch and water; stir into the Chop Suey; mix and cook till the sauce is thickened. Serve with hot rice. 4 to 6 servings.

FISH CHOP SUEY Substitute fillet of pike or sea bass, cut in small cubes, for the beef in Beef Chop Suey recipe. Add 1 or 2 thin slices green ginger, if you have it, to the oil, salt, and pepper in the hot skillet.

VEAL CHOP SUEY Substitute veal for pork in the Pork Chop Suey recipe.

PORK SUBGUM
CHOP SUEY

4 tablespoons cooking oil or
chicken fat
2½ teaspoons salt
½ teaspoon pepper
1½ pounds pork shoulder, cut in
1½-inch cubes
3 tablespoons soya sauce
1 cup celery, cut in pieces the
same size as the pork
1 cup diced onion
2 cups diced green pepper
2 cups diced green string beans
2 tablespoons molasses
3 or 4 cups boiling water or stock
1 cup canned or fresh bean
sprouts
½ cup diced canned water
chestnuts
1 cup diced fresh mushrooms
2 cups diced Chinese celery
cabbage
5 tablespoons cornstarch
½ cup cold water
½ tablespoon toasted almonds

Use large, heavy iron or aluminum kettle. Heat the oil, salt, and pepper; cook the pork 4 or 5 minutes, stirring to sear all sides. Add soya sauce and stir. Add green pepper and string beans; stir and mix. Add the molasses to the boiling water or stock. Pour over the meat and vegetables. Mix. Cover the pot and let cook over low heat 10 to 15 minutes, till the meat is done. Add bean sprouts, water chestnuts, mushrooms, and celery cabbage. Mix. Cover the pot and cook 10 minutes or longer. Mix cornstarch and cold water. Stir into the Chop Suey. Use large, heavy spoon; lift and mix and stir till the sauce is clear. Serve with hot rice. Garnish the top with a few almonds. 8 or more servings.

VEAL SUBGUM CHOP SUEY   Substitute veal for the pork in the above recipe.

SHRIMP SUBGUM CHOP SUEY   In place of pork in the Pork Subgum Chop Suey recipe, use 1 pound fresh shrimp, cleaned and diced.

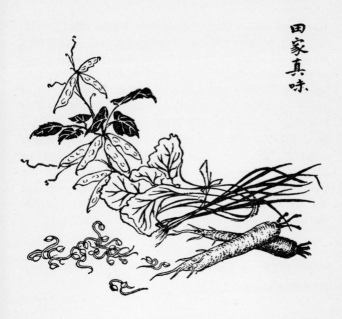

田家真味

Vegetables

田家真味

BROCCOLI
SAUTÉ

1 pound broccoli
3 tablespoons cooking oil
1 teaspoon salt
2 tablespoons soya sauce
1 teaspoon gin
1 teaspoon sugar

Wash broccoli; slice in thin diagonal pieces 1½ inches long. Cook the broccoli in the hot oil and salt, uncovered, 5 minutes. Stir and cook 2 or 3 minutes more. Mix soya sauce, gin, and sugar; pour over the broccoli. Add ¼ cup hot water. Cover. Bring to boiling point and cook 2 or 3 minutes. 4 servings.

CABBAGE SAUTÉ Use green cabbage in the above recipe; add 1 more teaspoon sugar.

CHINESE
BEAN SPROUTS

2 cups shredded beef
4 tablespoons cooking oil
1 sliver garlic
2 teaspoons salt
½ teaspoon mashed green ginger,
   if obtainable
4 cups canned or fresh bean
   sprouts, rinsed and drained
2 tablespoons soya sauce
½ cup stock or water
3 teaspoons cornstarch mixed
   with
4 tablespoons cold water
2 or 4 scallions, cut in 1-inch
   pieces

Cook the beef 3 minutes in the hot oil with garlic, salt, and ginger (if used). Remove the beef to a hot plate. Add the sprouts, soya sauce, stock or water. Bring to boiling point and cook 3 or 4 minutes. If thickening is used, add and stir till thickened. Add scallions. 4 servings.

Note: A small amount of any meat or poultry may be used to flavor bean sprouts, as in the above recipe. Or the sprouts may be cooked without meat, in oil, with the rest of the ingredients as directed.

CHINESE CELERY CABBAGE WITH SHRIMP

½ pound fresh shrimp
4 tablespoons cooking oil
1 teaspoon salt
2 tablespoons soya sauce
1 pound Chinese celery cabbage, cut in 1-inch pieces

Shell, clean, and wash shrimp; cut a gash down the back of each. Heat oil and salt; sauté the shrimp till pink. Add soya sauce; stir. Add celery cabbage; mix. Cover the pan and bring to boiling point. Stir and cook 2 or 3 minutes. 2 or 3 servings.

BOK CHOY

1 bunch (1½ pounds) bok choy vegetable, or use Chinese celery cabbage or American cabbage
6 slices lean bacon, cut in 1-inch pieces
½ teaspoon salt

If you can shop at Chinese grocery stores and find bok choy, wash it, then cut it crosswise in 1-inch pieces.

Drain. If you use Chinese celery cabbage, cut in 2-inch pieces; if the American cabbage is used, cut in 1½-inch squares.

Cook the bacon in a hot pan till brown; add the vegetable and a little salt. Stir from time to time. Cook 2 minutes. The celery cabbage contains a good bit of water, is delicate, and cooks quickly. Serve as vegetable. 4 servings.

> *Note: Either vegetable may be cooked in 2 or 3 tablespoons cooking oil in place of bacon fat. Or use ham in place of bacon and add 2 tablespoons cooking oil.*

CHINESE SNOW PEAS

1 pound Chinese snow pea pods or very young, tender pea pods
3 tablespoons cooking oil
1 teaspoon salt
½ cup boiling water

Wash pods; drain. Heat oil and salt; stir in pea pods. Add boiling water; stir. Cover and cook 2 minutes. Stir, cover again, and cook 1 or 2 minutes. 4 servings.

> *Note: Fully grown pea pods cannot be used, only the very immature, tender pods.*

CHINESE
STRING BEANS

> 1 pound young string beans, cut
> slantwise in 1½ or 2-inch
> lengths
> 2 tablespoons bacon fat, chicken
> fat, or cooking oil
> 1½ teaspoons salt
> 1 cup boiling water

Wash beans; drain. Add fat and salt to boiling water.
Add the beans and stir over high heat till boiling point.
Cover and cook 5 to 7 minutes. 4 servings.

STRING BEANS
AND
CHINESE CHEESE

> 3 cubes (tablespoons) Chinese
> Cheese (Foo Yee)
> 4 tablespoons cooking oil
> 1 pound string beans, cut in
> 1½-inch lengths
> ¾ cup hot water

Add the cheese to the hot oil in a large frying pan or
kettle; stir and mash the cheese. Add the beans; stir
and mix till the cheese is melted. Add the hot water;
mix. Let come to boiling point, lower the heat, cover,

and cook 2 minutes. Stir, cover, and cook 4 minutes or longer if well-done beans are preferred. Serve hot. 4 servings.

BOK CHOY AND CHINESE CHEESE   Wash Chinese bok choy; cut in thin diagonal pieces about 1½ inches long. Follow directions in above recipe. Cook till vegetable is tender.

SPINACH AND CHINESE CHEESE   Wash spinach thoroughly; drain; chop coarsely. Follow directions for String Beans and Chinese Cheese.

WATERCRESS AND CHINESE CHEESE   Wash watercress thoroughly; drain; cut off any coarse stems. Follow directions for String Beans and Chinese Cheese, but cook watercress less.

**STRING BEANS
AND EGGS**

2 cups fresh string beans, sliced
 slantwise in 1-inch pieces
2 cups boiling water
2 tablespoons cooking oil
1¾ teaspoons salt
1 slice bacon, cut in ½-inch pieces

3 eggs
1 or 2 tablespoons soya sauce

Wash and drain beans; cover with boiling water. Add the oil and 1 teaspoon salt. Cover and bring to boiling point. Cook 2 to 3 minutes; drain off water. Cook bacon in a deep frying pan; pour off half the fat. Add beans and the remaining salt; stir and cook 2 or 3 minutes. Beat the eggs slightly, pour over the beans; stir 1 or 2 minutes. Pour soya sauce over and serve. 2 or more servings.

MUSHROOMS
WITH BEEF

1 pound fresh mushrooms
Boiling water
¾ pound beef, cut in thin strips
6 tablespoons cooking oil
1 teaspoon salt
2 tablespoons soya sauce
1 tablespoon gin
2 tablespoons cornstarch
¼ cup cold water

Wash the mushrooms; drain; remove stems. Cover mushrooms with boiling water and let stand 2 or 3 minutes. Drain; cut mushrooms in halves. Sauté the beef in hot oil; add salt; stir and cook 2 or 3 minutes. Add soya sauce and gin mixed together. Stir and cook 1 or 2 minutes; stir in mushrooms; add ½ cup boiling

153

water; cover and cook on low heat about 2 or 3 minutes. Add the cornstarch mixed with cold water. Stir till sauce is thickened. Serve hot. 2 to 4 servings.

SAUTÉED
WATERCRESS
WITH PORK

4 bunches watercress
2 tablespoons salt
¾ pound chopped pork shoulder
4 tablespoons cooking oil
1 sliver garlic
2 tablespoons soya sauce

Wash and drain watercress; cut off any heavy stems. Fill a large pan with cold water; stir the salt into it. Add the watercress; let stand 20 minutes. Drain. Rinse thoroughly under running cold water. Drain very dry. Sauté the pork in hot oil with the garlic. Cook till browned and done. Add the soya sauce, mix. Add the watercress. Stir, cover, and cook over low heat till boiling point. Stir again. Cover and let boil 2 more minutes. Stir and serve. 2 to 4 servings.

SAUTEED WATERCRESS WITH BEEF Use beef in place of pork. When beef is cooked, remove it from the pan. Add the watercress and cook as described. When done, add the beef, stir, and serve. 4 servings.

154

青
紅
色
香

Sauces

青
红
色
香

OYSTER SAUCE   If you cannot shop in a Chinese grocery store for the popular Oyster Sauce, you can make a good oyster sauce in your own kitchen as follows:

> 1 dozen fresh or quick-frozen oysters, chopped fine or ground
> 1 cup oyster liquid
> 3 tablespoons soya sauce
> 1 teaspoon salt
> 2 teaspoons molasses
> 1 tablespoon flour
> 1½ tablespoons water

Heat the oysters in the liquid; cover the pan and cook over low heat 20 minutes. Let cool a little, then press through a sieve. Mix with the soya sauce, salt, and molasses. Let simmer over low heat 20 minutes. Add flour and water mixed together. Stir till thickened. Pour in bottle and keep in refrigerator. Makes about 2 cups sauce.

HOT MUSTARD SAUCE Use very hot dry English mustard. Add a little water at a time to the dry powder. Stir till sticky and thick; add more water, gradually thinning to a sauce consistency.

The longer it is stirred the hotter the sauce. Better flavor is developed if you mix at least ½ cup of mustard powder at a time. Add water, about 1 teaspoon at a time, stirring steadily, till very thick. Then dilute to desired consistency.

> *Note: To keep it for some time, first boil the water, let it cool, and use as described.*

PLUM or "DUCK" SAUCE

> 1 cup plum jelly
> ½ cup chutney (Major Grey type) chopped very fine
> 1 tablespoon vinegar
> 1 tablespoon sugar

Beat all together smoothly. Serve with Egg Rolls, Fantail Shrimp, Lobster, Barbecued Spareribs, Chinese Roast Pork, or almost any dish. 4 servings.

This sauce and Hot Mustard Sauce are usually served in two small dishes, with Egg Rolls and other favorites.

SUBGUM GINGER Preserved ginger is available in jars in Chinese grocery stores and at many other grocery shops. It is served as relish or garnish and is added to some sauces or sweet-and-sour dishes.

Desserts & Sweets

SESAME
SEED CAKES

  2 cups sifted flour
  ½ teaspoon baking powder
  ½ cup strained melted lard or
     beef suet
  ½ cup sugar
  2 eggs
  ½ cup sesame seeds
  2 tablespoons water

Sift the flour and baking powder together into a bowl.
Make a hollow in the center, pour in lard or suet,
sugar, and 1 egg, beaten. Work all together with your
fingers till a soft dough is formed. Use a very little
water if necessary. Knead and work the dough gently
till smooth. Turn out on a lightly floured board, shape
in a long roll about ½ inch thick. Cut off ½-inch pieces;
roll each lightly into a ball; press flat on a greased
cookie tin. Beat the remaining egg yolk with water
and brush the cookies lightly with it; sprinkle them

163

with sesame seeds. Brush lightly with the slightly beaten egg white. Bake in a moderate oven (350° F.) 15 minutes. 24 or more cookies.

ALMOND COOKIES

> 1 cup rice flour
> ½ cup brown sugar
> 2 cups blanched almonds, ground
> ⅓ cup butter, softened
> 24 to 36 small roasted almonds

Sift rice flour and sugar together. Mix with the almonds. Work the butter smoothly into the mixture. Add a few drops of water if needed to hold the dough together.

Shape in small balls; place on a greased cookie sheet, leaving plenty of space around each. Press an almond in the top of each. Bake in a moderate oven (350° F.) about 15 minutes, or till golden brown. Makes 24 to 36 cookies, according to size.

CHESTNUT BALLS

> 2 quarts chestnuts
> ½ cup honey or thick cream
> 1 cup powdered sugar
> 1 cup thick sugar syrup

Steam or boil chestnuts till shells burst; remove shells; grind the nuts as fine as possible, or put through ricer. Moisten with a little honey or cream. Shape in balls the size of a walnut and roll in powdered sugar, or dip in thick sugar syrup and let cool. 20 or more servings.

TO MAKE THE SYRUP, boil 2 cups sugar, 1 cup boiling water, ⅛ teaspoon cream of tartar. Boil without stirring till syrup begins to darken. Remove the pan from heat; set it in a large pan of cold water. Dip chestnut balls in, coat lightly, and place on waxed paper to dry.

CHINESE PEANUT CANDY

1 cup brown sugar
1 cup sugar syrup (or light corn syrup)
1 cup peanuts
½ pound puffed rice
¼ cup sesame seeds, dried in a warm oven 5 minutes
Butter for pan

Cook sugar and syrup together till a little dropped into a cup of cold water forms a hard ball. Spread the peanuts, puffed rice, and half the sesame seeds in a buttered pan. Pour the syrup over; sprinkle remaining sesame seeds on top; let cool. Break in pieces. Makes about 1 pound.

PLUM
CONSERVE

6 pounds blue plums, weighed
after they are quartered and
seeds removed
4 pounds granulated sugar
½ pound blanched almonds,
chopped
1 cup preserved ginger, ground
Grated rind 4 oranges
Juice 1 orange

Wash plums; cut in quarters; remove seeds; weigh fruit and place in an enamel preserving kettle. Add other ingredients, and cook uncovered slowly 2 or 3 hours, or until as thick as marmalade. Pour in sterilized jars. Store in cool place. 8 or more pints.

GINGERED
PEARS

8 pounds ripe pears
½ pound preserved Canton
ginger and its syrup
4 pounds sugar
4 lemons or 6 limes

Wash pears; peel, quarter, and core. Slice thin into an enamel preserving kettle. Grind the ginger; add sugar, ginger and ginger syrup in layers. Cover and let stand

overnight. In the morning grate the rind of 2 lemons
and add to pears, then peel the white from all lemons,
quarter and seed them; cut into small pieces; add to
pears. Cook slowly, uncovered, 3 hours, or till thick as
marmalade. Fill sterilized jars. Seal and store in a cool
dry place. 8 or more pints.

PRESERVED QUINCES

> 2 quarts cooked quartered
> quinces and juice (quinces
> peeled and cored)
> 1 cup seedless raisins
> 1 cup chopped blanched
> almonds
> 5 cups sugar

Place all ingredients in an enamel preserving kettle.
Bring to boiling; reduce heat and cook slowly, uncovered, till thickened and clear. Fill sterilized jars;
seal; store in cool, dry place. 4 or more pints.

PRESERVED KUMQUATS

> 3 pounds fresh kumquats
> 1 quart boiling water
> 1 pound granulated sugar
> 1 cup preserved ginger, ground
> Juice 2 limes

Wash kumquats; stick each in several places with a darning needle. Place all ingredients in an enamel preserving kettle. Cook slowly till the liquid is thick and clear. Seal in sterilized jars. 5 or more pints.

沽酒自當爐
三餐費思量

Menus

沽
酒
自
當
爐

三
餐
蓴
思
量

CHINESE DISHES IN AMERICAN MEALS

If you have eaten Chinese cookery only in Chinese-American restaurants, your idea of a Chinese meal probably is Chop Suey, or Chow Mein, or Egg Foo Young, with rice and tea, and an almond cookie and ice cream served afterward as dessert.

But if you have dined with Chinese-American friends in their homes, or if you have visited my homeland and been a guest of a Chinese family, you know that the pleasure and satisfaction of dining Chinese style are something quite different from the simple menu mentioned above.

The elaborate home meal of many foods is served in China as a ceremonial of friendship and sociability. At such a meal the dishes of food and sauces are always placed in formal arrangement on a beautiful table. Small dishes contain our famous sweet-and-sour sauces. Larger dishes contain rice and the fish, duck, meat, and other delicious foods. Appetite appeal, nourishment, and good flavor are the qualities the Chinese host provides for his friends.

Such a meal, of so many and such varied foods, is not usual or practical for most American homes. I hope my friends who use this book will quickly learn to enjoy our dishes by selecting their favorites from it and serving them as featured delicacies for their guest and family dinners.

When you plan a Chinese dinner, I suggest you begin with a savory appetizer, or a soup, and then serve only two or three of our delicate and satisfying main dishes, but try to balance it by serving a variety of foods and flavors—not too much of one kind. Also serve one or two of the savory hot or sweet-and-sour sauces which do so much to round out the flavor interest in Chinese dining.

If you must serve a sweet of some kind as dessert, see the menus at the end of this chapter for suggestions. This is not true Chinese style; we eat few sweets, and never after a meal.

For a simple meal omit soup or appetizer; serve one delicious dish and rice and tea, and your family and guests will consider themselves well fed.

The recipes I have included in this book are all adaptable to American kitchens and appetites. Some of them call for ingredients which can be found only in Chinese grocery stores of large cities. Or they are sold under Chinese-importer labels all over America. But most of the recipes can be prepared with the foods you grow in your garden, or which you buy at the corner market and grocery store—this is the aim of this book. Some of the seasonings will be found at the corner drugstore, at an herb shop, or health food store, if not in the grocery store.

At first you may think there is a lot of work entailed in the preparation of a Chinese meal, because the vegetables must be carefully sliced in thin, slant-wise pieces, or diced fine, or cut in equal lengths; and the meat must be cut in thin shreds, or diced, and other details of preparation are different from most American cookery.

But you will find that nearly all of the foods are quickly cooked, much more quickly than the average American dish. Chinese taste demands that only the youngest, most tender vegetables are used, and these are cooked only two or three minutes, not long enough to take away the garden freshness.

Meat, fish, chicken, duck, turkey, and squab are cooked barely enough to turn the fresh rawness into juicy, savory flavor.

Soups are delicate, clear or thickened, served in small amounts, to whet appetite and prepare the hungry stomach for the more filling foods which follow.

The economy and ease of preparation of most Chinese recipes please any homemaker, and these foods feed her family well.

For added atmosphere and interest, use Chinese bowls and other dishes for soup, rice, and other foods. These can be bought in Chinese stores as well as gift shops. Their shapes and colors add beauty and color to the table. Use a sensible, large pottery teapot and small handleless cups, so easy to pick up, for sipping hot tea during the meal. These add to the pleasure of the occasion.

Recipes for all dishes in the menus are given in this book.

TWENTY-THREE MENUS

Watercress Soup
Barbecued Spareribs
Chicken Lo Mein
Preserved Fruits
Tea

Butterfly Shrimp
Plum Sauce   Mustard Sauce
Rice
Beef with Bean Sprouts
Almond Cookies
Tea

Corn Chowder with Crushed Chicken
Egg Rolls
Mustard Sauce   Plum Sauce
Beef and Tomato with Green Pepper
Rice
Tea

Chicken Livers Sauté
Shrimp Fried Rice
Beef and Broccoli
Tea

伍

Tomato Egg Drop Soup
Rice
Beef Curry with Onions
Sesame Seed Cookies or Candy
Tea

六

Chicken Broth and Noodles
Fan-tail Shrimp
Plum Sauce
Rice   Smooth Chicken
Tea

175

Savory Chicken Wings
Rice
Shrimp Cantonese Style
Bok Choy
Tea

Beef Vegetable Soup
Rice
Almond Diced Shrimp   Chinese String
    Beans
Thin Rice Flour Cookies
Tea

Fringe Pike
Rice
Beef with Ginger
Broccoli Sauté
Almond Cookies
Tea

Egg Foo Young
Rice
Chinese Celery Cabbage with Shrimp
Tea

Deep-fried Chicken Livers
Eggs and Crab Meat Sauté
Rice
Almond Cookies
Tea

Chicken Broth and Rice
Sautéed Watercress and Pork
Pot Roast Chicken and Mushrooms
Rice
Tea

Egg Rolls   Plum Sauce
Chicken Soup Yatka Mein
Tea

177

十四

Shrimp with Tomatoes and Green Pepper
Rice
Tea
Preserved Fruits
Cookies

十五

Crabs Cantonese Style
Rice
Bok Choy
Tea

十六

Barbecued Spareribs
Steamed Sea Bass
Rice
Almond Cookies
Tea

十七

Flounder in Savory Sauce
Rice
Chinese String Beans
Tea

Egg Cube Soup
Sweet and Sour Shrimp
Rice
Tea

Celery Cabbage Soup
Beef and Broccoli
Rice
Preserved Fruits
Tea

Savory Chicken Wings
Beef with Ginger
Chinese Green Peas
Rice
Tea

Chicken Broth with Rice
Sweet and Pungent Pork
Broccoli Sauté, or Bok Choy, or New Cabbage
Rice
Tea

#二

Egg Roll or Fan-tail Shrimp
Plum Sauce   Mustard Sauce
Chop Suey
Rice
Tea

#三

Chicken Broth with Rice
Subgum Chicken Chow Mein
Preserved Fruits
Tea

SUGGESTED SUBSTITUTES

In all Chinese cooking peanut oil is used. However,
you may use any kind of cooking oil or any brand of
vegetable oil.

Fresh ginger root is commonly used, but if this is un-
obtainable, powdered ginger may be substituted. If this
is not available, it may be omitted from the recipe.

Fresh bean sprouts are obtainable only from a Chinese grocery store, but you may use canned bean
sprouts, as there are several brands available in most
grocery stores.

Bamboo shoots come canned, and many American grocers carry them. However, you may use fresh rutabaga just as well. But first remove the skin, then slice ¼ inch thick. In fact, you may use this vegetable in place of various vegetables, and even make a delicious soup with it.

Water chestnuts. Naturally fresh ones are better, but they also come canned. Here you may substitute rutabagas also, but cook slightly in order to maintain crispness.

Fresh noodles or fried noodles. Fried noodles may be bought canned. However, you may use packaged egg noodles. Soak the noodles in boiling water first, till soft, and then in cold water for five minutes. If used as a side dish, they may then be browned in slight amount of oil in frying pan. If to be served *under* the main dish, frying may be omitted, but the noodles should be boiled, drained, and dried out by shaking over low heat.

Bok Choy, an original Chinese vegetable, usually is found only in Chinese stores. Therefore, you may substitute any one of many vegetables if you can't buy it—such as celery cabbage, fresh new cabbage, Swiss chard, broccoli, rutabaga, celery, or young white turnips.

Chinese snow peas—originally from China and transplanted in Long Island, N.Y., Florida, California, Arizona, and other parts of the country. These are usually sold only through Chinese merchants. The nearest thing is the American pea pod, but this must be very young and used before the peas even show inside the pod. Otherwise they would be very tough and stringy.

Soya sauce. This is more or less common and carried in most groceries. When it is used as a seasoning, in addition to being used as a condiment on the table, care must be taken not to use too much salt, for soya sauce, in addition to its flavor, is very salty itself.

Soft-shell crab and hard-shell crab. If you are using hard-shell, remove meat from shell and then proceed as with the soft-shell recipes.

Cooking time given in the recipes is based on the boiling-point start. When recipes say "simmer" or "lower heat," that means a very slow heat, barely enough to bring up to boiling point.

Anyway, I trust you use your common sense and apply it to all recipes.

索引

INDEX

索引

186